D0216342

CAMBRIDGE MUSIC HANDBOOKS

Janáček: *Glagolitic Mass*

CAMBRIDGE MUSIC HANDBOOKS

GENERAL EDITOR Julian Rushton

Cambridge Music handbooks provide accessible introductions to major musical works, written by the most informed commentators in the field.

With the concert-goer, performer and student in mind, the books present essential information on the historical and musical context, the composition, and the performance and reception history of each work, or group of works, as well as critical discussion of the music.

Other published titles

Bach: Mass in B Minor   JOHN BUTT
Beethoven: *Missa solemnis*   WILLIAM DRABKIN
Berg: Violin Concerto   ANTHONY POPLE
Handel: *Messiah*   DONALD BURROWS
Haydn: *The Creation*   NICHOLAS TEMPERLEY
Haydn: Six String Quartets Op. 50   W. DEAN SUTCLIFFE
Mahler: Symphony No. 3   PETER FRANKLIN

Janáček: *Glagolitic Mass*

Paul Wingfield
Trinity College, Cambridge

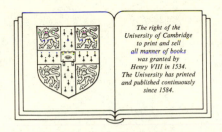

The right of the
University of Cambridge
to print and sell
all manner of books
was granted by
Henry VIII in 1534.
The University has printed
and published continuously
since 1584.

Cambridge University Press
Cambridge
New York   Port Chester
Melbourne   Sydney

Published by the Press Syndicate of the University of Cambridge
The Pitt Building, Trumpington Street, Cambridge CB2 1RP
40 West 20th Street, New York, NY 10011–4211, USA
10 Stamford Road, Oakleigh, Victoria 3166, Australia

© Cambridge University Press 1992

First published 1992

Printed in Great Britain at the University Press, Cambridge

A cataloguing in publication record for this book is
available from the British Library

Library of Congress cataloguing in publication data
Wingfield, Paul.
Janáček, Glagolitic Mass / Paul Wingfield.
p.   cm. – (Cambridge music handbooks)
Includes bibliographical references (p.   ) and index.
Discography: p.
ISBN 0 521 38013 8 (hardback). – ISBN 0 521 38901 1 (paperback)
1. Janáček, Leoš, 1854–1928. Mša glagolskaja.
I. Title. II. Series.
ML410.J18W56   1992
782.32′3 – dc20   91–16986   CIP

ISBN 0 521 38013 8   hardback
ISBN 0 521 38901 1   paperback

CE

To Elizabeth

My Mass will be quite different from all the rest . . . I will show people how to talk to God.

Leoš Janáček

Contents

Contents

Acknowledgements

Most of this book was written while I was a Research Fellow, first at the University of Sydney and then at Gonville and Caius College, Cambridge; I would like to thank both the Rothmans Foundation and Caius for financial support during that period. I am also grateful to the Royal Musical Association for funding my purchase of a microfilm of Václav Sedláček's copy of the *Glagolitic Mass*, which is housed in the Österreichische Nationalbibliothek in Vienna; and to the Schweizerische Landesbibliothek in Berne for providing me with photocopies of Janáček's correspondence with William Ritter.

In Brno, I am indebted to Jiří Sehnal and Svatava Přibáňová of the Music History Division of the Moravian Museum, and to Alena Němcová of the Czech Music Information Centre – without their advice and assistance my research in Czechoslovakia would not have been nearly so fruitful. I am very grateful to Julian Rushton for suggesting the book and for his invaluable comments at the draft stage. Penny Souster deserves special thanks for her alert editing and her patience during the final months of the book's genesis. Finally, I wish to thank John Tyrrell, whose encouragement and example have influenced many of the pages that follow.

Note on musical examples, bar numbers, abbreviations and translations

In musical examples tempo and metre markings are shown in three ways:

(1) without brackets: Janáček's marking at that point in the score;
(2) in brackets: the composer's marking earlier in the score;
(3) in square brackets: editorial.

Bar numbers apply to the printed Universal full score, except for the fourteen bars cut from the 'Svet' during the rehearsals for the first performance and reinstated by me (Example 8); these are allotted lower-case roman numerals (i–xiv).

The following abbreviations are used. In Chapter 2, 'OCS' and 'CS' denote 'Old Church Slavonic' and 'Church Slavonic' respectively. In the chapters about the music, chords are sometimes represented by roman numerals. Arabic numbers are often appended to these numerals to indicate inversions and added notes; additional sharp and flat signs denote the raising or lowering of a note or triad by a semitone. Also, major and minor triads are frequently distinguished by upper-case and lower-case roman numerals. Hence, in C major, 'I', 'ii', 'bIII' and '♯iv' represent triads of C major, D minor, E♭ major and F♯ minor. Actual pitches are usually referred to by capital letters; where necessary, they are pinpointed further by the Helmholtz system, in which c^1 is middle C and each octave is deemed to rise from C to B.

All English translations from Czech, French and German are by Paul Wingfield.

Introduction

Janáček's *Glagolitic Mass* (1926; revised 1927) dates from towards the end of the final, exultant phase of his compositional career. Begun when he was seventy-two, this Mass constitutes the peak of a remarkable sustained burst of creative energy encompassing the eight years following the First World War, a period in which he also completed three operas – *Kát'a Kabanová* (1919–21), *The Cunning Little Vixen* (1921–3) and *The Makropulos Affair* (1923–5) – as well as the Sinfonietta (1926) and several chamber pieces. After a short break the Mass was followed by two further major works: *From the House of the Dead* (1927–8) and the Second String Quartet (1928). This late flowering of Janáček's old age helped him to achieve a degree of international fame that would have seemed incredible to him ten years earlier.

The composer's rapid rise to prominence and astounding productivity in his last decade owed much to the enthusiastic reception of the 1916 Prague premiere of his opera *Jenůfa* (1894–1903). First performed in Brno (his home town) in 1904, this opera took twelve years to reach the more cosmopolitan Prague stage. During his frustrating wait for recognition, a disillusioned Janáček finished only a modest number of works. The 1916 premiere precipitated a sudden improvement in his fortunes. Universal Edition acquired the rights outside Czechoslovakia for the score of *Jenůfa* and initiated performances in Vienna and several German cities. Equally importantly, Max Brod (1884–1968), the leading Prague-based German novelist and critic, wrote an extremely complimentary review of the opera and translated its text into German. Brod became a zealous promoter of Janáček's music, translating the song cycle *The Diary of One Who Disappeared* (1917–20) and all the composer's subsequent operas apart from *The Excursions of Mr Brouček* (1908–17). Buoyed up by his belated success, Janáček now completed several projects started half-heartedly before the War and embarked on a whole series of fresh ones.

I

Other factors that contributed to Janáček's Indian summer of concentrated compositional activity were his new mood of optimism engendered by the recently acquired independence of his country and his friendship with Kamila Stösslová (1892–1935), the wife of an antique-dealer in Písek, Bohemia. Janáček probably met Kamila, thirty-eight years his junior, for the first time in the Moravian spa town of Luhačovice in 1917. He rapidly became enamoured of her and, though she did not reciprocate his feelings, he wrote to her regularly for the rest of his life. In his more than 700 letters to Kamila he ascribes to her the inspiration of several of his works including the *Diary* and *Kát'a*.

The *Glagolitic Mass* is undeniably one of Janáček's most renowned non-operatic works, but church music in general forms only a minor part of his oeuvre. In addition to a few Czech hymn harmonisations and some organ pieces, he wrote about a dozen small-scale sacred compositions with Latin texts and four in the vernacular, the slightly more substantial *Moravian Our Father* (1901; revised 1906), and three masses. Of the masses, the first (c. 1872) is lost and the second (1907–8) is an unfinished didactic setting in the *Missa brevis* style. Thus the *Glagolitic Mass* is Janáček's sole major composition with a sacred text. Furthermore, this work, with its large orchestra and substantial proportion of purely instrumental movements and interludes, is designed for the concert hall, not for liturgical use.

One reason why Janáček's cultivation of music for the church was so limited was his attitude towards religion. Despite having spent some of his formative years in an Augustinian monastery, he was agnostic as an adult. He expressed scepticism about the existence of God many times, declaring in print that he would make up his mind only when he could see for himself (p. 120), and he refused extreme unction on his deathbed. Unsurprisingly, therefore, he was drawn most frequently to texts on erotic, natural or patriotic themes.

Janáček's neglect of sacred music was also a manifestation of the decline of liturgical composition in the nineteenth and early twentieth centuries. In this period church music became increasingly the province of minor composers, while the relatively few settings of sacred texts by important figures such as Liszt and Verdi were conceived as grand works for concert performance. The gulf between church music and contemporary mainstream developments was widened further by the Cecilian movement. The aims of this movement included the promotion of a strictly functional role for ecclesiastical music, a return to the *a cappella* polyphonic style of the sixteenth century and the banishing of orchestral instruments from churches. Cecilian principles were expounded by prominent clerics and musicians in the eighteenth and early nineteenth centuries, but they were not put into practice until the second half of the nineteenth. The German church musician Franz Xaver Witt (1834–88) was mainly responsible for the implementation of Cecilian reforms in German-speaking countries and the dissemination of the movement's theoretical precepts further afield. In 1869 he was the principal founder of the Allgemeiner Deutscher Cäcilien-verein, an organisation which was awarded the sanction of the Holy See the following year, and which encouraged the setting up of many sister societies throughout Europe. Despite the less extreme stance adopted towards instrumental participation in the liturgy by a later leader of the movement, Franz Xaver Haberl (1840–1910), Cecilianism exerted a stranglehold on Catholic church music well into the twentieth century, an ascendancy that was reinforced in 1903, when Pope Pius X's *Motu proprio* discouraged the orchestral mass.

The musical activities of the Cecilian movement clearly helped to deter Janáček from writing regularly for the church, but the text of his *Glagolitic Mass* is to a certain extent a product of the Czech strain of Cecilianism. In the Czech lands the movement's leading pioneer was Ferdinand Lehner (1837–1914), who founded a periodical entitled *Cecilie* in 1874. In addition to historical studies, catalogues of sacred polyphony etc., this publication printed short compositions in the restrained Cecilian style by such composers as Josef Cainer (1837–1917), Josef Foerster (1833–1907) and his son Josef Bohuslav Foerster (1859–1951). From the initial stages, Czech Cecilianism assumed a patriotic orientation. In particular, it became associated with research carried out by scholars of linguistics into the first liturgical language of the Czech lands, Old Church Slavonic, and its two scripts, Cyrillic and Glagolitic. This language had been introduced into what is now Moravia by the ninth-century missionaries Constantine (Cyril) and Methodius, but had been supplanted in the West Slavic region by Latin when the Roman rite was imposed on that part of Europe after Methodius's death in AD 885. Modern study of Old Church Slavonic began with the Czech scholar Josef Dobrovský's *Institutiones linguae slavicae dialecti veteris* (1822), but it was not until the Croat Vatroslav Jagić published his important editions of two major Old Church Slavonic codices in 1879 and 1883 that it was finally possible to separate this language from later accretions. Jagić's first edition coincided with one of the earliest manifestations of the rise of Czech 'Cyrillism' (as the nationalistic reinterpretation of Cecilianism has been labelled): the establishment in 1879 by Lehner in Prague of a music society called the Ecumenical Cyrillic Union. In the same year the journal *Cecilie* was renamed *Cyrill* (later *Cyril*), though its musical content changed little in style.

As knowledge of Old Church Slavonic increased and the influence of Cyrillist ideas spread throughout Bohemia and Moravia, scholars began to compile missals which, while adhering to the format of the Roman Catholic rite, were mainly written in a later Croatian variant of Old Church Slavonic employing Glagolitic characters. In the early years of this century transliterations into Latin letters of the Ordinary of the Mass from these missals had become available in printed editions. The transliterations soon began to interest composers influenced by Cecilian/Cyrillist ideals. For example, in c. 1920 Karel Douša (1876–1944) wrote his *Missa glagoljskaja* Op. 21a for unaccompanied mixed chorus; and in 1923 J. B. Foerster produced his *Glagolská mše* Op. 123 for chorus and organ. Both these works are designed for liturgical use and are Cecilian in their modest scope and understated idiom. Their performance in church was made possible by a Papal edict in 1920 permitting the celebration of the Roman rite in Church Slavonic in certain Czech churches on major feast days, such as those of St Wenceslas (28 September) and Sts Cyril and Methodius (7 July).

Janáček's composition of a *Glagolitic Mass*, which post-dates those of Douša and Foerster, is therefore on one level a consequence of the patriotic linguistic and liturgical researches connected with the Cyrillist movement. That Janáček shared the partly nationalistic motivation, if not the musical objectives, of the Cyrillists is also evidenced, for example, by the specifically Czech inspiration behind his first five operas. Another influence on his decision to set a Church Slavonic text was his espousal of the pan-Slavic concept of a union of all the Slav peoples, an idea which was admittedly always more important as a symbol than a concrete political aim. From the days of his youth Janáček regarded Russian as the key modern Slav tongue, and he studied it throughout virtually his entire adult life. Moreover, he based several instrumental works and his operas *Kát'a* and *From the House of the Dead* on Russian literature. But since Church Slavonic in its earliest form was close to Proto-Slavic, the common ancestor of all living Slav languages, this was in principle an even more satisfactory linguistic medium for the expression of Janáček's pan-Slavic sympathies.

Of course, Janáček's Mass is very different in scale and musical conception from its Cecilian counterparts. Its starting-point is the nineteenth-century concert mass with vocal soloists, large chorus and full orchestra, as exemplified by Liszt's *Missa solemnis* (1855; revised 1857–8) and

Hungarian Coronation Mass (1867). Like Verdi's Requiem Mass (1874), its style is dramatic, even operatic in places. Furthermore, it is much more significant historically than the earlier Glagolitic masses: its early performances outside Czechoslovakia meant that it played a part in the general European revitalisation of sacred art music, for both concert and liturgical performance, by prominent composers after the First World War, a rejuvenation which embraces such works as Vaughan Williams's Mass in G minor (1920–1), Poulenc's Mass (1937), Kodály's *Psalmus hungaricus* (1923), *Budavári Te Deum* (1936) and *Missa brevis* (1942–5), and Stravinsky's Mass (1944–8). Above all, Janáček's *Glagolitic Mass* surpasses its predecessors in terms of sheer imagination. Its highly original musical language and its unique combination of elements from West and East European liturgical traditions have earned it justified and widespread acclaim as a masterpiece of the twentieth-century choral repertoire.

Genesis and reception

Composition and revision

The origins of the *Glagolitic Mass* go back to before the First World War, as do those of some of Janáček's other late works – for example, the String Quartet No. 1.[1] In 1907–8 the composer began to draft a Latin Mass in E♭ for mixed chorus and organ. He dictated this unfinished piece to his composition pupils at the Brno Organ School in spring 1908 as an example of how to set a sacred text. Janáček wrote only a Kyrie, an Agnus and about two-thirds of a Credo. He then put the work aside, returning to it in 1926, when he reused much of it in the first draft of the *Glagolitic Mass* and afterwards destroyed his score of the earlier piece.

The Latin Mass has been preserved owing to the endeavours of Vilém Petrželka (1889–1967), a Czech composer who had been a Janáček pupil in 1908. Just before Christmas 1942, fourteen years after Janáček's death, Petrželka reassembled the work from his own transcript and those of some fellow ex-students of the composer, and at the beginning of 1943 he completed the Credo. Petrželka then orchestrated all three movements. In 1946 Hudební matice of Prague published the individual parts for Petrželka's completion of the choir and organ version. The full score, in preparation when Hudební matice was closed down in 1949, was eventually issued jointly by Supraphon of Prague and Bärenreiter of Kassel in 1972.[2]

Examples 1 and 2 demonstrate the close relationship between the Latin and Glagolitic masses. They show bb. 1–5 of the printed score of the 1908 Kyrie and a transcription of the corresponding section of the initial draft of the 1926 'Gospodi'. Although Example 2 contains a motive (in the two solo female voices in the last three bars of the excerpt) not employed in the 1908 Kyrie and already identifiable as the principal motive of the published 'Gospodi' of the *Glagolitic Mass*, it does incorporate all the music in Example 1 with minimal alterations. In fact, the entire 1908 Kyrie

Ex. 1

provides the framework for the first draft of the expanded 1926 movement. Many ideas from the 1908 Credo and a substantial part of the Agnus were also reused in the initial drafts of the equivalent movements ('Věruju' and 'Agneče') of the later work.

Janáček's revisions of the *Glagolitic Mass* removed literal quotations from the earlier piece. Nevertheless, the published versions of the two works still contain some striking correspondences on various structural levels. For example, the opening *a cappella* phrases of the 1908 Agnus and 1926 'Agneče' are similar: each contains a *crescendo* and ends with a downward fall of a second in an inner part. On a larger scale, both movements juxtapose mainly unaccompanied homophonic choral statements with an intermittent instrumental ostinato.

Ex. 2

Ex. 2 *continued*

According to Petrželka, Janáček said to his pupils when dictating the 1908 Mass: 'Write Latin, but think Czech' (Vogel 1963, 147). This remark suggests that, nearly twenty years before the *Glagolitic Mass* was composed, the possibility of setting a Slavonic Mass text had occurred to him. However, it was not until 1921 that this idea was developed further. Father Josef Martínek, also once a Janáček pupil, writes (Vogel 1963, 317):

It was perhaps at the beginning of the school year 1921–2 when Janáček . . . said to me that in the holidays he had met Archbishop [Leopold] Prečan . . . in Hukvaldy . . . Janáček told the Archbishop that he had been to a nearby church and that the music there had been feeble . . . To his talk of a decline in church music the Archbishop said: 'Well, maestro, you should compose something worthwhile'. Janáček . . . did not want to set a Latin text: 'If only I could get hold of an Old Church Slavonic one' . . . I told him that this would be easy, since I had the Old Church Slavonic text, in fact two copies of it . . . Both copies were the same, but the text published in *Cyril* [1920], a church music periodical, was

9

edited by [Josef] Vajs, an authority on the Old Church Slavonic liturgy. The accented syllables of each word were printed in bold type. I recommended this text to him and lent it to him, so that he could copy it out for himself. The *Glagolitic Mass* was composed to this text.

Even if Janáček acquired a Church Slavonic text in 1921, it was another five years before he began his musical setting. In the intervening period he was busy with *The Cunning Little Vixen* and *The Makropulos Affair*, as well as with his 1924–5 revisions of his early opera *Šárka* (1887–8). He also wrote two chamber works – *Youth* (1924) and the Concertino (1925) – and the Sinfonietta, which was completed on 15 May 1926 (Wingfield 1987b, 100–1).

In June–July 1926 Janáček sketched and drafted his Capriccio for piano left hand and wind. Towards the end of July he put this piece to one side and at last turned his attention to the Church Slavonic text supplied by Martínek. He made some brief sketches and then left for Luhačovice, where he often spent part of his summer vacation. There he wrote an entire draft of the Mass between 2 and 17 August, drawing substantially on his Latin Mass of 1907–8. At this stage the work had seven movements arranged in the draft in the following order: 'Úvod' (Introduction), 'Gospodi' (Kyrie), 'Slava' (Gloria), Intrada, 'Věruju' (Credo), 'Svet' (Sanctus) and 'Agneče' (Agnus). The initial three movements of the draft were written between 2 and 9 August, the next three were finished by 15 August and the 'Agneče' two days after that.

Having completed the draft, Janáček wrote to his wife on 17 August: 'I am still missing from that Mass *the printed Cyrillic text* and many pages of sketches. We found some – but that is not all of them. I have done a lot of work here and I would like to get the rest off my hands quickly when I return.' (Večerka 1957, 64). Obviously, Janáček had departed hurriedly for Luhačovice, leaving some material behind. The reference to a printed text perhaps suggests that he did not return Martínek's *Cyril* copy in 1921, or that he obtained a duplicate in the period 1921–6. The fact that he managed to draft the work in Luhačovice without this printed text indicates that he took his own handwritten copy of it with him – possibly his 1921 transcript – and, indeed, of the two manuscript texts corresponding to the *Cyril* version that have survived, one is in Janáček's hand and seems to date from no later than 1926. In addition, the composer does not appear to have been too inconvenienced by his mislaying some sketches, so either these contained ideas already rejected or he was able to remember their content when he compiled his draft. (Few early sketches for the work are now extant; a page of jottings for the 'Slava' is reproduced in Racek 1975, Plate 14.)

Once he was back in Brno Janáček set about acquiring a replacement printed text. On 31 August he wrote to Václav Mikota, the director of Hudební matice, asking for help (Vogel 1963, 317). Mikota passed on Janáček's request to several likely contacts. On 2 September Jaroslav Dušek, the chief editor of *Cyril*, sent the composer a copy of Josef Vajs's article 'Masses in Honour of the Patron Saints in the Old Church Slavonic Language' from a 1921 issue of that periodical. The following day Hudební matice wrote to inform Janáček that his request had been referred to a Canon V. Müller, who was consulting the Christian Academy in Prague about the matter. Janáček was sent a further communication the very next day (4 September), this time by Emil Kubíček, the Rector of the Papal College at the small, but historically important, South Moravian town of Velehrad. In addition to his letter, Kubíček included 'some' (only one survives) Church Slavonic Mass texts transliterated into Latin characters, which he claimed to have taken from a missal in the Archiepiscopal Archive in the larger nearby town of Kroměříž.

Janáček selected a text sent by Kubíček as a temporary model. This was another Vajs transliteration, from a missal published in Prague in 1919. On 5 September the composer began the first revision of his Mass, which now acquired a title, *Misa slavnija (Missa solemnis)*. The first part of the title was taken from the 1919 missal, the second from Beethoven's *Missa solemnis*, a work which Janáček had conducted in Brno as early as 1879. While Janáček was compiling his second draft, Dušek finally sent him on 14 September another copy of the 1920 *Cyril* text, which he now used alongside his 1919 model.[3] In his second version of the Mass, which also had seven movements, he made many structural alterations within movements and moved the Intrada to the very end of the piece. As soon as the second draft was finished Janáček wrote a fair copy, his third and final draft, which incorporated some extra, less extensive revisions. At this point the work was renamed *Missa glagoljskaja (Missa solemnis)*, the first part of this title coming from Douša's Op. 21a, a copy of which Dušek had sent to Janáček with his letter of 14 September. Janáček finished his autograph score on 15 October, nearly three months after he had written his preliminary sketches for the Mass. He then gave his fair copy to the flautist Václav Sedláček (1879–1944), his main copyist in the 1920s. After that, Janáček turned his attention once more to the Capriccio, revising his initial draft in the last two weeks of October.

The 'Varhany solo' (Organ Solo) of the *Glagolitic Mass* was drafted and revised at some point between 30 October and the beginning of December. On 31 October Janáček declined a commission for a piece for chorus and organ from the Singers' Union of Moravian Teachers, remarking in a letter to this society that, although the organ 'is the most godlike musical instrument', he was already using it 'in its proper place'.[4] These comments do not make it clear whether Janáček had begun the Organ Solo by this date, or whether the commission actually inspired the creation of that movement.

Sedláček finished his score in early December. Janáček then gave him the Organ Solo to copy, along with instructions for this movement to be inserted between the 'Agneče' and the Intrada. The composer also made minor alterations in the 'Slava' and the 'Věruju' and rewrote the final two pages of the Intrada, changes which were inserted into the copy itself by Sedláček, who used paste-overs where necessary. The second layer of the Sedláček score was finished on 20 December. After that, Janáček, an inveterate polisher, altered bb. 105–10 of the Organ Solo, Sedláček again inserting the corrections into his copy by means of a paste-over.

Once he had supervised the revision of Sedláček's score, Janáček put the Mass aside. On 28 December he commented in a letter to Max Brod: 'My mind has never been so empty of ideas before now . . . Ordinarily, as I am finishing one work I am already starting another.' (Racek and Rektorys 1953, 211). It was not until February 1927 that Janáček began a new work, the opera *From the House of the Dead*, to which he devoted most of his time in the next three months (Tyrrell 1980, 4). His interest in the *Glagolitic Mass* was reawakened in early May 1927, when a performance was arranged for the following December. Prior to the copying of the parts Janáček altered the title again, this time to *Misa glagoljskaja (Missa solemnis)*, and modified all the movements apart from the Organ Solo. Most of the alterations concerned the orchestration, dynamics and expression markings, but some important structural revisions were made: for example, the opening motive of the 'Úvod', previously played by only the trumpets, was reworked imitatively between the trumpets and horns. On this occasion Janáček inserted all the changes himself into Sedláček's score.

The copying of the parts occupied at least three copyists for more than two months. These parts were considered lost until April 1987, when I discovered several of them in the archive of the Brno State Philharmonic Orchestra. This archive holds more than twenty chorus parts, five parts for the first violins, three for the second violins, and two each for the violas, cellos and double basses. All the first violin parts, one for the second violins and one for the violas were the work of the orchestral player Jaroslav Kulhánek, who initialled them. (Kulhánek wrote a number of copies for Janáček in the 1920s, including one of the Concertino.) The remaining extant parts were written by two unidentified copyists, neither of whom worked regularly for the composer. Kulhánek's parts are all dated, forming the following chronological sequence: 29 May; 11, 19, 26 and 29 June; 6 and 31 July.

Before the start of August Janáček made some pencil revisions in the Sedláček copy. These altered the timpani part in the 'Úvod' and the 'Slava', in addition to creating the whole of the soprano part in bb. 3–14 of the 'Slava'. Since the numerous corrections in the Sedláček score had now made it rather untidy, Janáček gave it at the beginning of August to Kulhánek to act as an exemplar for a second, more legible authorised copy. Kulhánek finished this new full score on 1 September.

Although Janáček seems to have considered the *Glagolitic Mass* to be ready for performance once the Kulhánek copy was completed, he later made several hundred revisions in November and December 1927, continuing to revise the piece until just before the premiere. These last-minute emendations appear to originate from the time after Janáček began attending the rehearsals. Regular practices for the chorus alone were held from September 1927 onwards in the Besední dům ('Friendly Society House') in Brno; Vilém Blážek (a Janáček pupil in 1920–4) was the repetiteur and Jaroslav Kvapil the conductor (see Blážek 1969, 684). In November the four vocal soloists began attending these rehearsals, and Janáček himself went for the first time on 18 November. According to Blážek, the composer made many alterations between and even during practices. For instance, in a rehearsal at the end of November Janáček added a new solo alto part in bb. 35–7 of the 'Agneče', this singer having until then been allotted a meagre seven bars.

Janáček designed the majority of the initial November 1927 changes sketchily in pencil in the Sedláček score, amplified them in black ink, and then expanded them further in red ink. The emendations were then copied more neatly into the Kulhánek score largely in red pencil (a few in red ink) and the orchestral and choral parts were modified in both black ink and blue pencil. Despite the complicated nature of these revisions, the composer was apparently still not satisfied. He now wrote in black ink yet more alterations in the Sedláček score, which were swiftly reproduced in the Kulhánek copy and the parts also in black ink. Thus it is no exaggeration to state that the sources for the *Glagolitic Mass* contain so many different layers that they are probably the most complex surviving Janáček manuscripts.

Performance and reception to 1928; publication

On the morning of 23 November Janáček composed an article for the Brno daily newspaper *Lidové noviny* with the heading 'Glagolskaja missa' (a further variant of the piece's title), giving his own poetic and rather fanciful account of the work's genesis. This article (reproduced in translation on pp. 116–19) was printed four days later on 27 November.[5] In the meantime, Janáček wrote to Kamila Stösslová on 25 November describing the piece in pantheistic terms (Štědroň 1953, 615; English translation on p. 119). The following day he sent a letter to Archbishop Leopold Prečan, the dedicatee, inviting him to the premiere of the Mass and acknowledging the important role that Prečan had played in its genesis (Blážek 1971, 113).

The orchestral rehearsals for the first performance began on Saturday 26 November. Three more ensued: 28 and 29 November, and 3 December.[6] The Swiss music critic and essayist William Ritter attended some of these rehearsals. A letter from Ritter to Janáček written on 17 December reveals that the first three practices were for orchestra alone, the vocalists joining the instrumentalists for the final one only two days before the concert.[7] During these rehearsals three final major changes were made: the abandonment of the use of three offstage clarinets in bb. 121–67 of the 'Věruju', the substantial revision of the 'Raspet' ('Crucifixus') section, and the removal of fourteen bars from the 'Svet'. Ritter was clearly impressed by what he heard at the final orchestral and full practices. Janáček reports in a letter to Kamila of 29 November that Ritter had told him the Mass was his best work.[8]

The premiere took place on the morning of Monday 5 December in the concert hall of the Sokol Stadium in Brno. The first part of the concert was devoted to another choral and orchestral piece requiring similar forces: Jaroslav Křička's Cantata *Temptation in the Wilderness* Op. 34 (1921–2), which had received its premiere in Prague on 25 November 1922. Both compositions were performed by the Chorus of the Philharmonic Club of the Brno Friendly Society and the Orchestra of the Brno Theatre, conducted by Kvapil. The soloists were Alexandra Čvanová (soprano), Marie Hloušková (alto), Stanislav Tauber (tenor), Ladislav Němeček (baritone) and Bohumil Holub (organ).

By the time of the Mass's first performance Janáček was widely regarded by his compatriots as one of Moravia's leading composers and his international reputation was growing. The work was therefore assured of a positive reception. Jan Racek recalls the audience's reaction: 'Today I can still see a picture of the excited maestro and how youthfully he responded to the . . . noisy and wholly spontaneous ovation.' (1975, 41). The reviews were equally favourable. Gracián Černušák produced one for that evening's edition of *Lidové noviny*, in which he describes the Mass as 'daringly original'. Three days later, in a review for the Prague daily *Tribuna*, Racek praised extravagantly the originality of the work. Ritter, who attended the premiere, put forward his views in his letter to Janáček of 17 December:

> It was with a very great sadness that I found myself in Prague morally unable to retrace my steps to return to Brno . . . to attend another performance of that astonishing *Glagolitic Mass* . . . In spite of all I subsequently heard in Prague, my brain never ceased to be galvanised by the vestiges, the traces left in it by that first hearing . . . I am most anxious for the score to be published so that I may more readily find the most emotion-filled pages. Until a more complete study is finished, a first article will describe the unexpectedness of that first revelation . . .

Janáček replied to Ritter's letter on 27 December, modestly commenting: 'The way you write about my work makes me red-faced.'[9]

Soon after the premiere, arrangements were made for the Mass to be published by Universal Edition. Ludvík Kundera – a pianist and close associate of Janáček – was entrusted with the task of preparing the vocal score. Finding a German translator of the text was not so easy. Janáček's natural inclination was to turn to Brod. Not having been in contact with Brod for some while, he was circumspect at first, simply remarking in a letter of 27 December 1927: 'Where have you got to? . . . You don't even know that I have written a "Glagolskaja missa" and that it is much revered . . . It is being published by [Universal] Edition.' (Racek and Rektorys 1953, 228; Susskind 1985, 116). Brod replied on 29 December, writing that he was pleased to learn of the Mass's success (Racek and Rektorys 1953, 229). Janáček made a more direct approach in the New Year, attempting to see Brod on a visit to Prague on 10 January. Brod was in Berlin, so the composer had to leave a note stating: 'I wanted to talk to you about the translations of *Šárka* and the *Glagolitic Mass* . . . It is urgent. The *Glagolitic* is to be published by the end of March.' (Racek and Rektorys 1953, 229–30; Susskind 1985, 118). Brod responded on 13 January, the day after his return from Berlin, turning down both proposals because of lack of time and recent overwork. Shortly afterwards Janáček, himself fatigued owing to a bout of influenza, went to Hukvaldy (the village of his birth, where he owned a house) for a couple of weeks to recuperate. By the end of the month Universal had at last secured the services of another German translator, R. S. Hoffmann.

As well as having the Mass translated into German, Janáček also had his Church Slavonic text checked by an expert. After the first performance he requested the 'Philosophical' Faculty of Jan Masaryk University in Brno to recommend someone who could edit his text. The Dean of the Faculty, František Chodoba, arranged for the Prague professor of Slavonic Studies, Miloš Weingart, to carry out the revision, informing Janáček about this by letter on 21 December (Večerka 1957, 71). Weingart took six weeks to accomplish what proved to be an extremely problematic task. The 1920 *Cyril* version of the text, which was sent in a second manuscript copy to Weingart and was presumably intended as the model for the Universal print, was littered with errors and linguistic inconsistencies. On 7 February 1928 Weingart at last sent his revision to Janáček along with a copy of his text in Cyrillic characters, also returning the manuscript copy of the 1920 version and writing that he was sorry for the delay, which had been caused by the complex nature of the undertaking and by his having to consult Josef Vajs (the compiler of both Janáček's printed models) about a number of details (Večerka 1957, 71–2). Eleven days later Weingart sent the composer a copy of the text in Glagolitic characters. Weingart's revised, transliterated version was passed on quickly to Kundera, who set about emending his vocal score.

Weingart altered the title of the Mass to *Mša glagolskaja* and made many straightforward orthographic changes, which Kundera was able to insert immediately into his score. However, in several instances Weingart's revisions affected the syllable count of the text and Kundera could not incorporate these modifications without rewriting Janáček's music. To compound Kundera's difficulties, his score was overdue and Universal was pressuring him to submit it. Thus he was forced to send it to Vienna in only a partly corrected state. Once the score had been dispatched, Kundera wrote to Janáček detailing some (but not all) of the places where Weingart's revisions had produced an increase or decrease in the number of syllables; he also urged the composer to consult Weingart as soon as possible (this undated letter is published in Večerka 1957, 72–3). But Janáček, busy with *From the House of the Dead*, waited until 17 March to communicate with Weingart, and then he asked the professor about the modification of only one line of text in the 'Svet', which had been increased by two syllables. Weingart wrote back on 28 March, reaffirming that Janáček's version of this line did not make sense and suggesting a new wording that was grammatically accurate but also preserved Janáček's syllable count (Večerka 1957, 73). Unfortunately, by this point Kundera had emended and returned the proofs and publication of the vocal score was imminent. Even if the composer had sent a list of corrections to Universal, they would have been unwilling to alter the plates at such a late juncture. In consequence, none of Weingart's major textual revisions was included in the 1928 print.

In February–March 1928 four articles about the Mass were published (translated extracts from all four are given on pp. 119–20, 120, 120–1 and 121). The first, a review by Václav Kaprál published in February in *Hudební rozhledy*, highlights the pantheistic inspiration behind the work. During the same month a longer article by Kundera was printed in *Tempo*. Though the content of this is largely uncontroversial, much of it simply charting the course of the music, one sentence is provocative: 'Janáček, an old man, now a firm believer, feels with increasing urgency that his life's work should not lack an element expressing his relationship to God.' On 28 February the composer sent Kundera a terse and indignant postcard: 'No old man, no believer! You youngster!' (Štědroň 1976, Plate 54; Zemanová 1989, 124). In fact, Janáček was so irritated by Kundera's remark that he amplified his response in an interview he gave for *Literární svět*, which was published on 8 March.[10] Here he also emphasised the nationalistic aspects of the Mass, presenting it partly as a celebration of Czechoslovak independence from the Austro-Hungarian Empire. On Sunday 18 March Ritter's long-promised article appeared in the *Gazette de Lausanne*. Effusive and exaggerated in its expression, this piece nevertheless conveys a genuine and impassioned response to the Mass that is unmatched in the contemporary literature.

The second performance of the work, the last during Janáček's lifetime, took place in Prague on 8 April with the soloists, choir and conductor who had participated in the premiere, but with the Czech Philharmonic instead of the original Brno orchestra. Janáček attended this concert and was in Prague for the rehearsals from 5 April onwards. In a letter to Ritter dated 31 March the composer complains that the scheduled rehearsals are insufficient: 'The orchestra has only a single rehearsal before the general one. That is too few. I will be there, but I'm not sure that I won't run away.'[11] In the event, Janáček did not flee in embarrassment and critical reaction was once more favourable. Elated by his success, the composer wrote on 12 April an open letter to the Brno performers, thanking them for all their hard work (Černušák and others 1960, 12). The next month he commented in a letter to Brod of 17 May about the Prague performance: 'The "Mša glagolskaja" was well received; it is fierce.' (Racek and Rektorys 1957, 236–7).

While Janáček was in Prague, the vocal score was published only a few days behind schedule. Universal wrote on 6 April informing him that it had been issued, sending him a complimentary copy under separate cover on the same day.[12] The work was printed with a different German title, 'Festliche Messe', since it was claimed by the publishers that a strict translation of the original one would be meaningless to, and might deter, prospective German-speaking purchasers. The full score was not published until the beginning of 1929, several months after the composer's death on 12 August 1928. In 1930 the vocal score was reissued with Latin and English texts (neither underlaid), prepared by Weingart and Rosa Newmarch respectively. Weingart also corrected some, although by no means all, of the textual errors not put right in 1928 and provided a short introduction outlining the problems of producing an accurate Church Slavonic text and of fitting a Latin translation to Janáček's music.

Growing acclaim and recording: 1929–90

By the time he died, Janáček was regarded in his native country as belonging to the first rank among composers of his generation and many of his works had already entered the repertoires of the principal Czechoslovak choirs and orchestras. Between 1929 and 1945 the *Glagolitic Mass* was performed quite regularly in Brno and was revived elsewhere in Czechoslovakia. Four particularly influential Brno renderings took place during this period under Jaroslav Kvapil on 4 December 1933 (with the same forces as the premiere), 11 April 1938, 30 May 1940 and 30 March 1944 (to celebrate the ninetieth anniversary of Janáček's birth). In other parts of continental Europe and the United States Janáček's music had established a tentative foothold by 1928. For example, *Jenůfa* was produced in several (predominantly German) opera houses outside his homeland in his last decade and the Sinfonietta was championed by Otto Klemperer, who in 1927 conducted it in places as far apart as Berlin and New York. Moreover, Janáček's reputation amongst contemporary composers and critics was enhanced in the 1920s through performances of the Violin Sonata

(1913–21), the First String Quartet and the Concertino at International Society for Contemporary Music festivals in Salzburg (1923), Venice (1925) and Frankfurt (1927) respectively. Clearly, Janáček's last and most significant choral work was guaranteed at least a degree of international interest once the full score was published.

The first foreign performance of the Mass was given in German on 28 February 1929 at the Hochschule für Musik in Berlin under Alexander von Zemlinsky, the recently appointed principal conductor of the Hochschule choir. The enterprising inclusion of the Mass in the programme for Zemlinsky's inaugural concert as the choir's conductor was rewarded by positive critical comment, Walter Schrenk remarking that the Mass had secured 'a special place within the literature' (*Anbruch*, 11 (1929), 170). Less than six weeks later the work was sung abroad in Church Slavonic for the first time, at the ISCM Festival in Geneva (6–10 April). Jaroslav Kvapil directed his Brno chorus and the *Suisse romande* Orchestra. Even though some members of the audience seem to have found the piece incomprehensible (notably the British contingent), the reviewers acclaimed it universally as the highpoint of the Festival and praised the Czech singers. Erich Steinhard was extremely impressed by the powerful, operatic style of the Mass (*Der Auftakt*, 9 (1929), 114 – see pp. 121–2).

Performances in Rotterdam (autumn 1929) and New York (autumn 1930) succeeded the German and Swiss premieres. The New York concert, given at the Metropolitan Opera on the afternoon of 26 October 1930, was conducted by Arthur Bodanzky, who had also directed the first performance of *Jenůfa* in the USA six years previously. Janáček's Mass attracted a long review by Olin Downes in the *New York Times*. This article (see pp. 123–4) is patronising in tone and describes the work as 'partly incoherent', but it does extol the originality of Janáček's musical language.

The initial degree of success attained by the Mass was respectable, considering its many unconventional features and the technical difficulties it presents to performers. However, enthusiasm was short-lived: as the piece's novelty value wore off, subsequent hearings outside Czechoslovakia became much more sporadic. Nowhere was the Mass's progress towards enlightened recognition more tortuous than in Britain. The few concerts of Janáček's music here in the 1920s were organised by an indefatigable English promoter of Slavonic music, Rosa Newmarch, with the co-operation of Henry Wood, and it was these two who arranged the British premiere of the *Glagolitic Mass* in 1930. The piece was performed in Newmarch's English translation as part of a morning concert at the

Norwich Festival on 23 October 1930, with Wood conducting the Festival Chorus and the Queen's Hall Orchestra. Audience reaction was polite but unsympathetic; the reviews exhibit a mixture of bewilderment, condescension and outright hostility. The *Daily Mail* critic writes (24 October): 'Norfolk people, known for their placidity and reserve, were not to be expected quite to capture the spirit of boisterous Bohemian [sic] rustics . . . If any sort of religious occasion was suggested by the music it was perhaps the dedication of a new railway station.' Harold Truscott in the *Yorkshire Post* (24 October) is extremely supercilious: 'It [the Mass] has to be taken as the exuberant joy of a primitive folk on a popular festival.' (see p. 122). The sole assessment displaying any effort to understand it is made in the *Manchester Guardian* review (also 24 October): 'All one can do is to free one's mind as far as may be of any preconceptions of what music should be. If one succeeds in that, one is at the beginning of being impressed by the undisciplined bigness of this work.'

The Mass failed to make an impact at Norwich for various reasons. First, the performance was substandard. Even one of the work's harshest critics, Ferruccio Bonavia, admits that the choir was ill at ease with its unusual idiom and that there were many 'weak spots of organisation' in the orchestra's contribution (*Musical Times*, 71 (1930), 1081–2; an extract is given on p. 123). Second, Newmarch's English translation did not fit well with the music, a fact gleefully pointed out by the reviewers. Indeed, Newmarch unwittingly provided the critics with extra ammunition when she emphasised the piece's 'patriotic' aspects in her programme note (quoted on p. 122). But the overriding factor was the widespread distrust of contemporary European music in Britain at the time. Stereotyped prejudices were to dog the reception of Janáček's works here for more than another twenty-five years.

Before 1945 there were two London revivals of the Mass, both sung in English and broadcast by the BBC. The first concert, transmitted live from the new Maida Vale studio on the National Programme on 28 June 1935, was given by Wood and the BBC Chorus and Orchestra. This venture merited introductory articles by Hans Hollander in the *Radio Times* (21 June 1935, 13) and Michel-Dimitri Calvocoressi in the *Listener* (26 June 1935, 1088). Calvocoressi advocates a more balanced evaluation of the work's worth: 'Now perhaps it [the Mass] will be . . . judged not according to any general conception of what religious music should be, but just as it stands.' Despite this plea, the small amount of critical attention the broadcast received was unflinchingly negative. Just how ingrained was the resistance to the composer's output is shown by a review of the next BBC broadcast, given on the Home Service on 14 November 1943 by the Luton Choral Society and the BBC Chorus and Orchestra under Leslie Woodgate. In this review, the unashamedly opinionated W. R. Anderson writes: 'Janáček's "Slavonic Mass" (1926) is a queer affair, noisy, gustily amateurish, with a slapstick element which seems to me near lunacy.' (*Musical Times*, 85 (1944), 13).

The twentieth anniversary of Janáček's death in 1948 was the cue for a high-profile rendering in Czechoslovakia conducted at the 'Prague Spring' on 5 June by Rafael Kubelík. This was broadcast later in the year in several European countries, but it aroused minimal enthusiasm. In Britain, the Prague concert went out on 1 October on the Third Programme, the irrepressible W. R. Anderson encapsulating contemporary opinion here by remarking: 'His [Janáček's] "Festival Mass" still seems queer, melodramatic, nervy music, at moments almost auto-hysteric: music of infatuation rather than inspiration.' (*Musical Times*, 89 (1948), 339). The work did not fare any better when Kubelík conducted it in the USA in July 1952. Neither in 1952 did *Kát'a*, the first Janáček opera to be produced in Britain (Simpson 1982, 120–2). Even the first recording of the Mass, conducted by Břetislav Bakala (yet another former Janáček pupil) and released in 1953, barely helped to promote it, despite a positive review by Alec Robertson in *Gramophone* (October 1953, 152). The issuing of this record on two relatively expensive ten-inch discs did little to encourage the recalcitrant public to get to know the work. In 1954 there was another Janáček anniversary: the 100th of his birth. The *Glagolitic Mass* was performed to considerable acclaim on 14 October of that year at a Janáček festival in Brno under the baton of Václav Neumann. But elsewhere the work played only a small part in the low-key centenary celebrations of a composer who was still regarded by most as an eccentric.

The tide began slowly to turn in 1956. Universal republished the full score in a more extended print run and in a smaller format. This reissue of the Mass aided the rejuvenation of its fortunes, especially in German-speaking countries. The piece was given, for example, in Vienna on 17 March 1956 in Latin, apparently for the first time in that language. In addition, the availability of a cheaper pocket score meant an increase in sales and a wider international dissemination of the actual musical text. The re-release in 1957 of the Bakala recording on a less costly single twelve-inch disc was another step forward. This entered the collections of a broader range of record enthusiasts and attracted much more attention from reviewers, Malcolm Macdonald even going as far as to claim: 'This is tremendous music by a very great composer.' (*Gramophone*, August 1957, 109). A further advance was made in 1958, the thirtieth anniversary of Janáček's death. Jaroslav Vogel, Janáček's biographer, conducted the Mass on 20 October at a Janáček festival in Brno, attended by scholars and critics from the USA and all over Europe, who reviewed the work positively in a number of influential periodicals. Janáček's music in general was accorded even more serious attention when Vogel's biography was published the same year in German and in 1962 in English.

Enough interest had now been generated in the Mass for three new recordings to be made in 1963–4. The first (1963) was a Czech production, with Karel Ančerl as conductor, the other two were American and West German recordings, directed by Leonard Bernstein (1963) and Kubelík (1964). The Bernstein performance, sung in a haphazard form of Church Slavonic, was judged inferior by critics, its 'Hollywood' gloss on Janáček's idiom earning Malcolm Rayment's disapproval (*Records and Recording*, December 1965, 79), and its 'hectic' sound drawing adverse comment from Andrew Porter (*Gramophone*, February 1966, 402). However, the Czech and German recordings were both hailed as fine interpretations, each chorus and orchestra (if not the two quartets of soloists) receiving considerable praise. In 1964 there was a remarkably successful performance of the Mass at the Edinburgh Festival by Jaroslav Krombholc and the Prague National Theatre Chorus. The approbation that greeted this concert surpassed that accorded to any rendition in Britain so far. The Krombholc performance of *Kát'a* at the same Festival also marked a turning-point in the reception of that opera (Simpson 1982, 124).

By the end of 1964 a sizeable number of critics, professional musicians and concert-goers in Eastern Europe, Britain, West Germany and Holland viewed Janáček as a major figure of the early twentieth century and saw the *Glagolitic Mass* as one of the composer's most important works. During the next fifteen years the piece gradually achieved in Europe a yet more exalted status. In England, for example, it was performed to a substantial audience by the London Symphony Orchestra and Chorus in the Festival Hall under Christoph von Dohnányi on 6 July 1968 and in August 1969 it reached the Three Choirs Festival (at Worcester). At this point Universal stepped in to exploit the growing British market by issuing an alternative vocal score with underlaid English and Latin texts, the former compiled by Malcolm Rayment and replacing the old Newmarch translation. In 1970 the piece helped to catapult Andrew Davis to prominence, when on 18 November he took over from Eliahu Inbal at short notice, conducting the BBC Chorus and Orchestra in a performance that showed, according to Ronald Crichton, a grasp of 'the message of this original, savagely conceived music' that was astonishing, considering the limited time available for Davis to learn the score (*Musical Times*, 112 (1971), 55).

In 1972 the Mass was at last considered significant enough to be given at the Proms and in the same year it was included in the repertoire of the Royal Choral Society, who sang it in the Royal Albert Hall under Meredith Davis on 7 December. The latter performance was criticised for its disastrous experiment of accompanying the music with an incongruous dance sequence, but Adrian Jack summed up opinion of the Mass itself when he wrote: 'It would take a lot to quell the impact of Janáček's magnificent score.' (*Music and Musicians*, 21 (1973), 75). The first recording of the work with English forces was made in 1973, the Brighton Festival Chorus (singing in Church Slavonic) joining the Royal Philharmonic Orchestra under Rudolf Kempe. The reception of this rendering was extremely favourable, the orchestral playing attracting special commendation.

The general trend throughout the northern half of Europe and in some Communist European countries from 1964 onwards was for the Mass to be performed in the provinces, as well as in capital cities. The Royal Liverpool Philharmonic Chorus and Orchestra, for instance, gave a 'fiery' interpretation in January 1974 under Andrew Davis. Also, the piece was sung increasingly in Church Slavonic instead of English or German. Another indication of the Mass's greater box-office appeal was the fact that, in contrast with critics of the fifties and early sixties, reviewers now did not consider it necessary to preface their articles with long introductions explaining the work to their readers. In the 1970s the Mass was introduced to far-flung parts of the globe, perhaps the most noteworthy national premiere taking place during the extensive 1977 tour of Japan by the Czech Philharmonic under Neumann.

The widespread celebrations of the fiftieth anniversary of Janáček's death in 1978 allowed the burgeoning international reputation of the *Glagolitic Mass* to expand further. In fact, in 1978–9 the work was given in more than twenty countries, from Finland to the USA. Neumann conducted it in several European cities, his performance with the Czech Radio Choir and Czech Philharmonic Orchestra in East Berlin on 9 October 1978 eliciting an enthusiastic response. It was also revived at the Proms under Norman del Mar and at both the Three Choirs Festival (once again at Worcester) and the Edinburgh Festival. Even amateur performances were mounted, for example in England by the Colchester Institute (22 June 1979).

Surprisingly, none of the three records made in 1978–9 was very satisfactory. The earliest of these, of a live performance on 5 January 1978 in Prague conducted by Neumann, was 'exciting more for its sense of an occasion than for its actual sound' (John Warrack in *Gramophone*, October 1981, 593). A competent but unexceptional 1978 recording by the Slovak Philharmonic Chorus and Orchestra with Ladislav Slovák as conductor (not released here) made little impression. A further insipid Supraphon disc, with František Jílek directing mixed Prague and Brno forces, was not improved by its replication of an unfortunate feature of early Czech recordings: a side-break midway through the 'Věruju'. Much more important was the second reissue in 1978 of the 1953 Bakala recording. This version had by now attracted a large following, Robert Layton expressing his admiration: 'in terms of conviction and atmosphere, this performance is superb' (*Gramophone*, August 1978, 366).

Since 1979 the popularity of the *Glagolitic Mass* has continued to grow, although of course it currently occupies a different position in the musical life of each country in which it has been performed. In Czechoslovakia, it has throughout the 1980s formed part of the repertoire of more than one major orchestra every year and has been given in relatively minor towns (e.g. in Gottwaldov). Its reputation in West Germany, Holland and Britain has been consolidated firmly, with revivals not only in the capitals but also in many of the larger cities: Birmingham, Leeds, Bremen, Cologne, Frankfurt, Eindhoven etc. The work is now famous in Switzerland and Scandinavia. In the Soviet Union and other East European countries it has become well-known through performances by visiting Czechoslovak choirs and orchestras. Some non-European countries, such as Japan and Australia, have also been introduced to the work. Oddly, despite the fact that the Mass was first published in Austria and notwithstanding the 1956 Vienna revival, that country has lagged behind other German-speaking nations in accepting it. There was for a considerable time an analogous situation concerning English-speaking lands with the USA. After the initial performance of the piece there in 1930, its progress towards recognition was painfully slow and audiences stubbornly regarded it as a peripheral work until quite recently. Happily, the numerous renditions since the late 1970s in the original Church Slavonic have captured the imaginations of concert-goers and critics and the Mass has become a regular concert item on the other side of the Atlantic. In fact, of the developed nations, only the South European ones, and to a slightly lesser extent France, still view it more as a curiosity than as a mainstream composition.

Two new, influential recordings appeared in the eighties. The first digital recording of the Mass helped to launch the career of another young conductor, Simon Rattle, whose interest in the Mass went back to at least 1976, when he organised a performance at the Dartington Summer School. Some critics were disappointed, blaming many of the perceived shortcomings of the disc on the muddy acoustic of the Great Hall of Birmingham University, but others praised it, particularly for its 'convincing realisation' of the score's wide range of emotional nuances. In 1984 Charles Mackerras broke new ground in his Supraphon recording with Prague forces by restoring the deleted 'offstage' instruction in the clarinet parts in bb. 121–67 of the 'Věruju' and the fourteen bars cut from the 'Svet', changes which had been forced on Janáček during the 1927 rehearsals for the premiere. (Mackerras's justification for doing so is explained in detail in Chapter 3.) The true importance of Mackerras's discoveries was not appreciated by many reviewers, who concentrated myopically on comparing Supraphon's recording techniques with those of West European companies. However, other conductors have since followed Mackerras's practice, at least as far as the 'Svet' is concerned, notably Petr Vronský in two performances with the Brno State Philharmonic in April 1986.

In summary, the *Glagolitic Mass* has since 1956 gradually built up a worldwide, if uneven, reputation. It will never be performed as regularly as Janáček's other great large-scale non-operatic work, the Sinfonietta, on account of the practical difficulties caused by the unusual language of its text and the technical demands of its vocal parts. Nevertheless, today the Mass enjoys in many major musical centres a repertoire status that would have appeared impossible during the barren quarter-century following its British and American premieres.

2

The (Old?) Church Slavonic text

Introduction

The text in the published version of the *Glagolitic Mass* is in a hybrid and error-ridden transliterated variant of Old Church Slavonic (hereafter 'OCS'). In fact, as Miloš Weingart points out (1930), even the Mass's title is a misnomer, as the term 'Glagolitic' applies to OCS's original ornate script, which is abandoned by Janáček in favour of Latin letters. A correct name for the work as it stands would be 'Church Slavonic Mass'. It will qualify essentially for the appellation 'Old Church Slavonic Mass' after the printed text has been emended further. This chapter aims to identify problematic features of the Mass's text at each stage of its genesis and to suggest how the published text might be improved. A brief survey of the history of OCS provides the necessary background information. Then all versions of Janáček's text are examined in the following order: his printed 1920 and 1919 models; his various mixed texts in his sketches, two early drafts and autograph of the Mass; the partly modified texts in the two authorised copies, the manuscript parts and a 1928 transcript of the 1920 model; and Weingart's 1928 and 1930 revisions. The concluding two sections consider emendations suggested by Radoslav Večerka in 1957 and outline my own corrections. Table 1 (pp. 44–5) gives my complete, corrected text and an English translation. This table is followed by an OCS pronunciation guide for English speakers.

Although no linguistic jargon is employed in this chapter, one simple term – 'reflex' – may be unfamiliar to the reader. This label denotes a sound unit that corresponds to, or is derived from, another comparable form. Let us take as an example a word from the text of the *Glagolitic Mass*: 'krštenije' ('baptism'), which occurs in the 'Věruju' (see Table 1, line 50). The Bulgarian OCS form of this word is 'krštenije', whereas the Moravian OCS form is 'krščenije'. The word has the same meaning in both cases, but the Moravian version substitutes the reflex 'šč' for 'št'.

A brief history of Church Slavonic

All living Slavic languages and dialects are descended from Proto-Slavic, a Western offshoot of the Eastern Indo-European ('satem') group of languages. It took approximately three millennia for Proto-Slavic to evolve, beginning in c. 2000 BC. Even towards the end of the first millennium AD, the Slavic language was still essentially uniform in its grammar and phonology. Slavic literary endeavours began in the second half of the ninth century principally in the state of Moravia (now part of Czechoslovakia), which was a particularly important grouping of Slavic peoples at the time. In AD 862 the prince Rostislav of Moravia requested the Byzantine Emperor Michael III to send some missionaries to this region to give instruction in Christian law in the Slavic language. Michael nominated two suitably qualified brothers: Constantine, or Cyril (827–69), and Methodius (c. 815–85). Both men were natives of Salonica in Macedonia, which had a Slavonic-speaking population. They arrived in Moravia in the autumn of 863 (Dvorník 1970, 104), and they immediately set about translating parts of the Bible and other ecclesiastical texts from Greek into a generalised form of early Eastern Balkan Slavic, now known as 'Macedo-Bulgarian OCS', which was still very close to Proto-Slavic and readily comprehensible to all ninth-century Slavs.

In order to symbolise the independence of this first Slavic literary language, the missionary brothers composed for it a new, very individual alphabet called 'Glagolitic', from 'glagolŭ' meaning 'word'. The structure of this alphabet was Greek in origin, but the models for the shapes of many of its letters were certain Coptic, Hebrew and Samaritan characters, as well as non-alphabetic Christian symbols such as the cross and the triangle (Gardiner 1984, 12; and Auty 1960, 8).

By the time Methodius died in AD 885 the idea of using the mother tongue instead of Latin or Greek for cultural purposes had begun to permeate the whole Slavic world. However, the spread of OCS in the tenth and eleventh centuries was fragmented by wars, demographic movements and political realignments. To begin with, the Slavic peoples were gradually pushed into three distinct camps (East, South and West) by the incursion of the Magyars into what is now Hungary, by the Germanisation of the previously Slavic areas of Bavaria and Austria, and by Balkan Romanian expansion. Furthermore, after Methodius's death the Moravian mission was ended forcibly, German culture and its Latin liturgy becoming increasingly dominant in that locality. Some of Methodius's followers fled to Bohemia, where they maintained the Slavic liturgy in the face of mounting German opposition. But their influence waned steadily until, in the wake of the Great Schism of 1054 between the Western (Roman) and Eastern (Orthodox) Christian churches, Slavic monasteries were abolished in the region, the last disbanding in 1097 (Mareš 1985, 197).

On the demise of the Moravian mission, most of Methodius's followers went south to Macedonia and Bulgaria. In the Balkans OCS was modified, flourishing there for more than a century. To make it easier for educated Bulgarians and Macedonians (who spoke Greek as well as their own dialects) to read OCS, a less esoteric alphabet was devised for it. This alphabet, inconveniently named 'Cyrillic', is quite likely to have been the invention of St Kliment, a pupil of Cyril and Methodius (Lunt 1974, 14). Certainly, the Cyrillic script appears to post-date both the Glagolitic alphabet and the death of Cyril (Gardiner 1984, 12–13). More than half the Cyrillic graphemes were taken directly from Greek uncial letters, many of the remaining ones simplifying Glagolitic characters.

Slavic culture prospered in Bulgaria and Macedonia until both states were conquered by Byzantium in the period c. 970–1014. Even after that, the Slavic liturgy was preserved in Bulgarian, Macedonian and Serbian monasteries, as well as in Croatia (in the Western part of the South Slav region). But in the latter part of the eleventh century the creative centre of Slavic culture shifted to recently christianised Russia, where many Bulgarian and Macedonian intellectuals now migrated.

The small number of surviving OCS manuscripts and fragments date from a period of about 100 years starting at the end of the tenth century. Most are written in Cyrillic, a few in Glagolitic. They are probably merely copies of copies of ninth-century translations from Greek by Cyril and Methodius and their immediate disciples. The scribes who compiled them made many mistakes. Thus it is impossible to reconstruct the language of Cyril and Methodius completely.

In the tenth and eleventh centuries Slavic linguistic unity finally began to disintegrate, the various vernacular dialects developing many more independent characteristics. Reflections of the changes in these spoken forms of the Slavic language can be discovered in the OCS manuscripts, which have traits that are recognisably Bulgarian, Macedonian etc. The Bohemian/Moravian sources are even distinctive enough to justify our assigning a literary dialect of OCS to this particular region. The year 1100 has been accepted generally as a useful, if slightly arbitrary, date for the end of the OCS period. After that, non-Russian manuscripts are deemed to be written in one of four principal Church Slavonic (hereafter 'CS') 'recensions' (i.e. local critical revisions of the language): Bulgarian, Croatian, Macedonian and Serbian. Russian manuscripts are treated as a separate category, because even some of those from before 1100 have so many individual features that they can already be viewed as containing a Russian recension.

Perhaps the most important early phonetic mutations of regional Slavic dialects (reflected in varying degrees in OCS manuscripts) concerned the vowels '⟨ⱏ⟩' and '⟨ⱐ⟩' ('round' Bulgarian Glagolitic script; 'ъ' and 'ь' in Cyrillic). These sounds are often classified as 'reduced vowels', because they quite probably constitute shortened forms of the Indo-European normal short vowels 'ŭ' and 'ĭ' respectively (their exact phonetic values are unknown). Modern scholars prefer to label them 'hard jer' (pronounced 'yer') and 'soft jer' in accordance with their OCS spelling name, hence avoiding unwarranted precision. As early as the start of the tenth century the jers began to be dropped in 'weak' positions and to merge with different 'non-reduced' (full) vowels in 'strong' positions. In the main, a jer is 'weak' at the end of a word or in a syllable followed immediately by one containing a full vowel, and a jer is 'strong' in a syllable succeeded directly by one incorporating a weak jer. The dropping of jers was common to all Slav regions, but this development took place at different times in the various areas, progressing from the Balkans in the tenth century to the northern rim of the Slavic world not later than the second quarter of the twelfth (Lunt 1974, 30). In addition, the vowels that replaced the 'strong' jers were different in each locality.

Most OCS manuscripts evidence further dialectal phonetic changes. For example, in South Slav sources the nasal vowels '⟨ⱔ⟩' and '⟨ⱗ⟩' (Bulgarian Glagolitic), denoting the phonemes 'ę' and 'ǫ', are sometimes replaced by the reflexes (see p. 26) '⟨ⰵ⟩' and '⟨ⱆ⟩', indicating 'e' and 'u' sounds. Indeed, the use of nasal vowels even in relatively early manuscripts from these regions is so inconsistent that the sounds had obviously lost their nasality in the spoken dialects well before 1100. In Russian OCS sources the confusion of nasal and non-nasal vowel-letters is still greater, and in CS manuscripts graphemes representing nasal vowels disappear. Such phonetic modifications in post-1100 CS sources occur increasingly in conjunction with more and more distinct regional grammatical and lexical forms, indicating that local dialects were undergoing rapid, fundamental changes and separate Slavic vernacular languages were evolving.

Despite the growth of regional spoken languages, and though OCS had by 1100 fallen into disuse in West Slavic states (including Bohemia and Moravia) and in most of the Western Balkans, the five major CS recensions – Bulgarian, Croatian, Macedonian, Russian and Serbian – were the principal literary vehicles in these regions throughout the Middle Ages and beyond. The vernacular literary languages of the Orthodox and Croatian Catholic Slavs were formed by a tortuous process of emancipation from CS. From about 1100 onwards, Russia continued to lead in the propagation of CS. In fact, the full development of a Russian vernacular literary language was delayed until the eighteenth century.

In this century CS has persisted as a separate ecclesiastical language in several variants used by Orthodox Slavs and a few Croatian Catholics. As far as scripts are concerned, the simpler Cyrillic has triumphed almost everywhere over the Glagolitic. After about 1200 the Glagolitic alphabet was productive only in Croatia, where it was written in a more angular manner than elsewhere and was employed widely until the seventeenth century. There were isolated attempts in the fourteenth and fifteenth centuries by some Czech and Polish monastic communities to resurrect it, but these efforts soon petered out. Today, Glagolitic missals are still used by a few monastic communities on the Dalmatian coast of Croatia.

In conclusion, here are the opening words of Janáček's *Glagolitic Mass* – 'Gospodi pomiluj' – in Bulgarian 'round' Glagolitic script and in Cyrillic characters:[1]

(Latin)	G	O	S	P	O	D	I	P O M I L U J		
(Bulgarian Glagolitic)	Ⰱ	Ⰽ	Ⱄ	Ⱂ	Ⰽ	Ⰴ	Ⰻ	Ⱂ Ⰽ Ⰿ Ⰻ Ⰾ Ⱆ Ⰻ		
(Cyrillic)	Г	О	С	П	О	Д	И	П О М И Л ОУ И		

The printed transliterations

Clearly, Janáček's wish to set the Ordinary of the Roman Catholic Mass in 'the language of Cyril and Methodius' (see p. 118) was unrealistic. OCS as we know it is reconstructed on the basis of linguistic analysis of later copies of lost texts. The 'canonical' version of the language found in modern grammars and dictionaries is fundamentally eleventh-century, not ninth-century. In addition, there were further obstacles of a liturgical origin to the fulfilment of Janáček's aim. In ninth-century Moravia the liturgy appears to have been a mixture of Byzantine and Catholic (see Birnbaum 1981). No complete OCS missal has survived from this area, however.

Also, since the Liturgy in Bulgaria and Macedonia was Byzantine, there are no relevant OCS missals from that region either. It was in isolated Croatia that a Catholic Slavonic liturgy developed and, to make matters more complicated, the earliest surviving Croatian CS missal post-dates the Moravian mission by more than 400 years. Thus, even though it was not completely inappropriate for Janáček to try to set the Latin Ordinary in OCS, the textual models available to him in 1921–6 were several stages removed from the language and liturgy of Cyril and Methodius.

The first of Janáček's two models, the 1920 *Cyril* transliteration, was compiled by the Czech Josef Vajs from a missal in Glagolitic script, edited by the Croat Dragutin Parčić and published under the title *Misale Romanum slavonico idiomate e decreto ss. concilii Tridentini restitutum* (Rome, 1905). Parčić's missal was in turn based on the earliest extant Croatian Glagolitic missal, Vatican codex Illirico 4 (c. 1314–23). That manuscript has some lexical and morphological archaisms, but it belongs essentially to the later Croatian CS tradition.[2] The Vajs Latin transliteration of the basic Croatian Glagolitic text is problematic in three respects: it is (a) bewilderingly heterogeneous linguistically, (b) carelessly edited and (c) confusingly presented. Some (but not all) of Vajs's inconsistencies stem from the orthography of the Parčić missal and hence from Illirico 4.

To begin with, several Glagolitic characters are transcribed haphazardly. Vajs's representation of the grapheme ' Э' ('e') when it is used in his model as a substitute for the nasal vowel 'ЭС' ('ę') is especially confusing: it is replaced indiscriminately by the reflexes 'e', 'a' and 'ä'. Even worse is his illogical treatment of the jers. Hard and strong jers are frequently distinguished by the use of the common Macedonian and Russian reflexes 'o' and 'e', but sometimes both types of jer are rendered simply as 'e' (a custom in Czechoslovakia and some other regions). Equally unfortunately, Vajs vocalises some jers where they should not in fact be accorded sounding value. For instance, in 'въздаемъ' both jers (written here in Cyrillic script) are weak and should be dropped. Vajs's 'vozdajem' should thus be replaced by 'vzdajem' (Table 1, line 8). The abundant printing errors in the *Cyril* edition include the omission and displacement of diacritics and a host of orthographic mistakes: e.g. 'grěluj' should be 'grěhy' in Vajs's spelling system (Table 1, lines 13 and 14). Just as damaging is Vajs's mode of indicating his speculative stress patterns, which are based on modern Russian CS practice (precise details of OCS accentuation are unknown). Each stressed syllable is printed in bold type or has above it a Czech *čárka* (similar to the French acute accent). As the *čárka* normally indicates the lengthening of Czech vowels, its assignment to a different function here is unnecessarily confusing.

Janáček's other printed model, Vajs's 1919 transliteration, was published in a missal entitled *Misi slavnije o bl. Marii děvě i za umršeje obětnije slověnskim jezikom*. Also founded on the 1905 Parčić missal, this text differs substantially from the *Cyril* transliteration in orthographic terms. In fact, though it predates the *Cyril* text, it is preferable in some respects. It is slightly less diverse linguistically – employing only 'e' to represent the old nasal vowel 'ę', for example – and it contains fewer printing errors and no ambiguous indications of stress. But other features are less satisfactory, especially the use of the letter 'i'. In Illirico 4 and Parčić's missal one Glagolitic grapheme, ' ȣ ', is employed for the two OCS Glagolitic letters ' ȣ ' and 'ᚖ ᚗ' (Bulgarian script), denoting 'i' and 'y' (originally different phonemes). The 1920 Vajs text often (but not absolutely consistently) has 'i' and 'y' as etymologically appropriate, but the 1919 transliteration prints only 'i', thereby obscuring the etymology of the relevant words and simplifying the pronunciation. The use of the jers is also illogical in the 1919 text: it vocalises the same weak jers as the 1920 transliteration. In addition, the 1919 text's graphic representation of the jers is ambiguous. Hard and soft supposedly strong jers are replaced, according to Croatian CS tradition, by a single symbol, in this case 'ı' ('i' without the dot), presumably derived from the Croatian angular Glagolitic apostrophe ' ᛐ '. Vajs remarks in a note that Croats, Czechs, Russians etc. can interpret the sign according to their national practices regarding strong jers, Croats employing the reflex 'a' for both types, Czechs 'e', Russians 'o' and 'e', and so on. This is all very well, but the symbol 'ı' is difficult to distinguish from a normal 'i'; Janáček, to take the most pertinent example, treated 'ı' and 'i' as interchangeable when he consulted the 1919 text.

The texts in the sketches, drafts and autograph

Each of Janáček's versions of the *Glagolitic Mass* employs a different textual arrangement, the work's linguistic characteristics becoming increasingly diffuse. The few sketches that have survived and the now fragmentary first draft are based on the 1920 transliteration. The second draft (also incomplete) mixes the 1919 and 1920 models. Having mislaid his *Cyril* copy, Janáček received the 1919 text from Emil Kubíček on 5 September 1926 (see p. 11). The same day he began his second draft. Since the 'Gospodi' text has only three distinct words, the composer did not bother to consult the 1919 version when revising that movement, but he did base his second version of the 'Slava' on the 1919 text. On 15 September – having rewritten the 'Úvod', 'Gospodi' and 'Slava' – he received his replacement copy of the *Cyril* version from Jaroslav Dušek. He now reverted to that text for his revision of the 'Věruju' and 'Agneče'; but, with typical inconsistency, he used both models for his second draft of the 'Svet'. Thus in the 'Svet' even consecutive repetitions of some phrases appear in different variants.

The autograph is yet more hybrid textually. As in the second draft, the 'Gospodi', 'Věruju' and 'Agneče' are founded on the 1920 model, the 'Slava' mainly reproduces the 1919 version, and the 'Svet' mixes the two. A major problem concerning the autograph (and to a smaller extent the two earlier drafts) is Janáček's own reforming of the text. There are five types of intervention by the composer: errors; cuts; repetitions; changes of word order; and the introduction of modern Czech orthography and grammar. Mistakes range from the conflation of the words 'za ny' into a single word (Table 1, line 34) to the highly inaccurate phrase 'plna sut nebes i zem' in place of the 1920 version 'plna sut nebesa i zemlja' (Table 1, line 55). Omissions extend from one-letter words – the 'v' of 'v tretij den' (1920 form) is left out, for example (Table 1, line 36) – to whole groups of words. In all, six entire phrases are not set; in order of occurrence they are (in my orthography): 'Gospodi Bože, Cěsarju nebeskyj', 'Vzeml'ej grěchy mira', 'i včlověči se', 'pri Pontijscěm Pilatě', 'Osana vo vyšn'ich' (on its first appearance) and 'daruj nam mir' (Table 1, lines 9, 14, 33, 34, 56 and 61). As far as repetitions are concerned, we can ignore immediate restatements of text, but noteworthy are the reiterations of the opening word of the 'Věruju' as a refrain at various points of the movement and the insertion of supplementary statements of 'Amin' (my orthography) in bb. 19–24 of the same movement.

Janáček's two changes of word order occur in the 'Věruju': 'i našego radi spasenija' (1920) becomes 'i radi našego spasenija' and 'so slavoju sudit živym i mrtvym' (1920) is altered to 'sudit živym [i] mrtvym so slavoju' (Table 1, lines 31 and 40). Lastly, the intrusions of modern Czech forms are numerous. For example, the 1920 words 'jedin' and 'raspet' (Table 1, lines 16 etc. and 34) appear as 'jeden' and 'rozpet' (both spellings are closer to modern Czech) and some appearances of 'věruju' have been changed to 'věrujem', a pseudo-Czech first person plural form.

Most of Janáček's modifications seem unintentional, as the majority of them serve no meaningful purpose. They presumably crept in as the result of the compositional process. Concentrating purely on musical revisions in redrafts, Janáček would write out the text imperfectly from memory when composing the new versions of passages and would fail to check his text. Only two pairs of changes appear to have been deliberate: the omission of the first 'Osana' and the 'daruj nam mir'; and the reiteration of 'Věruju' and 'Amin'. Both omissions were made as early as the first draft, and in each of the relevant movements (the 'Svet' and the 'Agneče') the traditional musical forms were modified from the start. Similarly, 'Věruju' and 'Amin' appear to have been repeated for musical reasons. (See pp. 79 and 87 for details of the formal changes.)

The genesis of the text of the *Glagolitic Mass* reaches an apex of diversity in Janáček's autograph; in fact the most apposite title for the work at this stage of its development would be 'Pidgin Church Slavonic Mass'! From now on the history of the text involves attempts to clarify it.

The early textual revisions

Sedláček rectified several errors in the first layer of his 1926 copy. For example, the 'v' omitted from 'v tretij den' was reinstated and most modern Czech forms were removed. Presumably, Janáček gave him the 1919 and 1920 textual models, in addition to his autograph, as exemplars. Sedláček did not, however, make any corrections affecting the syllable count. His version was reproduced (mainly accurately) in Kulhánek's 1927 score. Thus Sedláček's revised text was sung at the premiere.

After the Mass's first performance two desultory attempts were made to improve the text further. The earlier, initiated by the composer and consisting of sketchy pencil annotations in the 'Slava' of the Sedláček score, brought the text into line with the 1920 *Cyril* version. The later involved the adoption of full Croatian CS orthography. (The instigator of these changes is unknown.) First, the *Cyril* text was copied out by hand with the Croatian jer reflex 'a' replacing 'o' and 'e' in three words. Then, pencil and ink annotations added many more Croatian spellings (further details in Večerka 1957, 70–1). Before the emendations were completed, this manuscript copy of the *Cyril* version was passed on to Miloš Weingart and the text of the Mass assumed a different orientation.

Weingart's alterations

Weingart's 1928 revision was far-reaching. In his letter of 7 February to Janáček (see p. 16 above), he censures the linguistic diversity of the Mass's text and points out that all the jers were pronounced at the time of Cyril and Methodius, also noting that to restore them would 'destroy' Janáček's 'musical phrases'. He then sets out the ground rules of his revision. As his model for content and word order he has used the most recent printed Croatian Glagolitic CS missal, edited by Josef Vajs and entitled *Rimski misal slověnskim jezikom: Missale Romanum slavonico idiomate* (Rome, 1927). Although using such a missal as a liturgical model was not ideal, Weingart had no alternative, because no OCS missal has survived.

For his actual orthography and grammatical forms Weingart drew 'as far as possible' on the generalised canonical reconstruction of Macedo–Bulgarian OCS. Therefore he employed 'i' and 'y' exclusively according to canonical OCS practice, several occurrences of 'i' in the Vajs text being converted to 'y' – e.g. 'Sinu' became 'Synu' (Table 1, line 12). Also, he altered two Bohemian/Moravian OCS reflexes used throughout Vajs's 1920 transliteration. In this West-Slavic OCS dialect 'z' and 'c' replaced Proto-Slavic '*d' ' and '*t' '. (The asterisks here are the standard symbols for unattested, reconstructed forms in Proto-languages.) Weingart restored in their place the Macedo–Bulgarian OCS reflexes 'žd' and 'št'. He also removed several Croatian CS features. For example, Vajs's 'Amen' became 'Amin' (OCS 'Aminъ').

A significant Weingart clarification of a different type was his modification of Vajs's orthographic depiction of the 'palatal' consonants 'l' ' 'n' ' and 'r' '. Palatal consonants are produced by placing the tongue against the front half of the roof of the mouth (the 'hard palate') while the consonant is articulated, a process which 'softens' the sound. In OCS 'l', 'n' and 'r' can either be hard or soft (palatal). Vajs indicated the palatal versions of these consonants by the clusters 'lj', 'nj' and 'rj'; Weingart chose 'l' ', 'n' ' and 'r' ', a method of transliteration which shows clearly that these were most probably single sounds, not clusters (Gardiner 1984, 19–21). The 'lj' etc. forms would mislead singers into enunciating 'l' and 'j' successively.

Weingart must have been tempted to restore the nasal vowels in his 1928 revision, as these were an important element at least of early Macedo–Bulgarian OCS. But he eventually decided to omit them, thinking that they would be too difficult for most singers. He contented himself with regularising Vajs's reflexes, always employing 'e' for 'ę' and 'u' for 'ǫ', in accordance with later Balkan usage. As far as the jers are concerned, Weingart decided that he had little choice in the matter. If all of them were to be reinstated as reduced vowels, in the region of 100 extra syllables would be added to the text of the *Glagolitic Mass*. Weingart observes

(1930) that the rewritings necessary to accommodate these syllables would 'rob' the work of its 'correct motivic and musical meaning'. Therefore he was once again satisfied with standardising Vajs's use of strong and weak jers. First, he converted consistently all strong hard jers to 'o' and all strong soft ones to 'e', Vajs's 'crkev' becoming 'crkov' for instance (Table 1, line 49). And second, he rectified Vajs's vocalisations of obviously weak jers, changing 'vozdajem' to 'vzdajem', for instance (Table 1, line 8). More straightforward were his corrections of orthographic errors and textual omissions – e.g. 'zany' was modified to 'za ny', 'živym, mrtvym' to 'živym i mrtvym' and 'životovorecago' to 'životvoreštago' (Table 1, lines 34, 40 and 43).

The net result of Weingart's alterations was a more consistent and fundamentally more archaic transliterated text. However, Weingart unfortunately failed to correct some Vajs and Janáček errors, and he added some mistakes of his own. Most seriously, he emended the bisyllabic endings '-žija', '-nija', '-niju' and '-nije' (occurring in a total of nine words) to the wrong monosyllabic forms '-žja', '-nja', '-nju' and '-nje'. It is not obvious why he did this. Vajs used the correct endings and Janáček retained most of these in his score, even if he did not allot a separate note to every syllable. Also misguided was Weingart's over-zealous removal of two more vocalisations of jers. He altered 'voskrse' to 'vskrse' and 'voskrsenija' to 'vskrsenja' (Table 1, lines 36 and 52). He was wrong, because in each of the OCS words 'vъskrьse' and 'vъskrьsenija' the first jer is strong and the second weak, so the Vajs forms should be kept.

Weingart's revision served as Kundera's exemplar for his 1928 vocal score. Kundera incorporated into his edition most of Weingart's corrections not affecting the syllable count. He also included one modification that did increase the number of syllables: 'slavy tvojej' became 'slavy tvojeje' (Table 1, line 55), although the extra syllable was not accounted for musically. However, on the whole, Weingart's emendations increasing or decreasing the syllable count were not incorporated. Instead, Kundera urged Janáček in his undated letter of late February/early March 1928 (see p. 16) to consult Weingart about these proposed alterations. Typically, Janáček followed up Kundera's request by writing to Weingart only about one correction: of the phrase 'plna sut nebes i zem' to 'plna sut nebesa [nominative plural] i zeml'a' (Table 1, line 55). In his reply, Weingart explains that Janáček's version violates basic grammatical rules ('nebes' is genitive plural, 'zem' does not exist) and writes that if the composer wishes to keep the same number of syllables he could substitute 'plna sut nebo [nominative singular], zemlja [sic]'. (Weingart presumably forgot that elsewhere he had denoted palatal 'l' by 'l'', not 'lj'.) His suggestion was ignored, because the proofs had already been corrected when Janáček received his letter. As a result, the texts in the 1928 vocal and 1929 full scores are highly inaccurate.

In his 1930 revision of the vocal score Weingart inserted 'plna sut nebo, zemlja' in bb. 45–6, 55–6, 70–1, 79–80 and 88–9 of the 'Svet'. He also reinstated the '-žija', '-nija', '-niju' and 'nije' endings, evidently having discovered his earlier mistake at some point since March 1928. He supported those changes by incompletely realised alterations of the voice parts in a total of sixteen bars: bb. 5, 14, 30, 33, 38 and 133–4 of the 'Slava'; and bb. 39, 72, 262, 264, 302, 357–8, 363 and 367 of the 'Věruju'. Example 3 shows Weingart's 1930 version of the relevant voice parts in

Slava, b.5 (similarly bb. 14 and 30)

Slava, b. 33 (similarly b. 38)

Slava, bb. 133–4

Ex. 3

37

Věruju, b. 39

Sy - na   Bo - ži - ja

Sy - na Bo - ži - ja

Věruju, b. 72

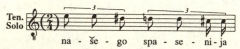

na - še - go   spa - se - ni - ja

Věruju, bb. 262–4

Pi - sa - ni - ju,   po   pi - sa - ni - ju,

Pi -   sa -   ni -   ju,

Věruju, b. 302

cě - sa - rstvi - ju

Věruju, bb. 357–8

Je - di - no kr - šte - ni - je   v o - tpu - šte - ni - je

Věruju, b. 363 (similarly b. 367)

vo - skr - se - ni - ja

Ex. 3 *continued*

38

these bars along with my editorial additions. Unfortunately, Weingart did not rectify any more errors in 1930.

The suggested 1957 emendations

In his 1957 article (p. 74) about the text of Janáček's Mass, the Czech Radoslav Večerka proposes some more changes. First, he notes correctly that 'chvali' (Table 1, line 8) should be 'chvaly', according to the etymology of the word. Second, Večerka observes that 'svět', meaning 'light', in Table 1, line 16, is wrong: it should be 'svet', meaning 'holy' (OCS 'svęt'). Third, he detects a Bohemian/Moravian reflex that escaped Weingart's scrutiny: 'šč', from Proto-Slavic '*st''. This occurs in two words, 'krščenije' and 'otpuščenije' (Table 1, lines 50–1) and it should give way in both instances to Macedo–Bulgarian OCS 'št'. In addition, Večerka puts right in his edition of the text (pp. 74–5) two more errors without explanation: 'za ny' appearing for 'zany' and 'zeml'a' for 'zemlja'.

One further suggested Večerka emendation is acceptable, but his reasoning is faulty. He comments that 'sj' in 'vsja' (Table 1, line 29) should be palatal 's', but then states that 'sj' can be replaced simply by hard 's', because singers would not be able to pronounce the palatal sound. In fact, there is no evidence that palatal 's' existed in OCS (see Lunt 1974, 25). In OCS manuscripts this word (meaning 'all') is 'vьsa', or more rarely 'vьsja'. Thus the printed version 'vsja' is feasible, even if 'vsa' might be preferred. Večerka's last proposal is misguided. He suggests that the word order of 'iže nas radi člověk i radi našego spasenija' become 'iže nas člověk radi i spasenija našego radi' (Table 1, lines 30–1) 'according to Church Slavonic custom', without demonstrating the musical realisation of this change. It is inconsistent to tamper with Janáček's word order here and not to do so in the phrase 'sudit živym [i] mrtvym so slavoju' (Table 1, line 40), which should be 'so slavoju sudit živym i mrtvym'. Also, in order to achieve both transformations, substantial musical emendations would have to be made. On balance, it seems most sensible to accord priority to the integrity of the music.

Additional proposed revisions

Before detailing some final necessary textual revisions, we must reconsider the awkward question of the jers and nasal vowels. Weingart did not restore the former simply because the extra syllables could not be fitted to the music without a complete revision of the voice parts, and he did not reinstate the latter because he decided that singers would find them difficult to pronounce. However, omitting the jers and nasal vowels can also be justified on linguistic grounds. Though Janáček wanted to write a work in the 'language of Cyril and Methodius', he actually set a hybrid CS text based on a manuscript from the fourteenth century. Weingart, realising that the composer's aim was impracticable, was more realistic in his revision: he simply tried to standardise this text according to the canonical reconstruction of OCS (based on mainly eleventh-century sources). If we accept, as did Weingart, that trying to get back any nearer to ninth-century OCS would involve too much speculation, it makes little difference whether the jers and nasal vowels are sung or not. For, despite the fact that these are included in OCS grammars and dictionaries, we know that in the eleventh century those sounds were pronounced increasingly rarely – jers were probably even dropped in the tenth century in Bulgaria. In consequence, if we retain only strong jers, ignore the nasal vowels, and ensure that Janáček's text is brought fully into line with reconstructed OCS in all other respects, we can view it as a transliterated approximation of spoken eleventh-century Macedo–Bulgarian OCS. The text will still not be absolutely in 'the language of Cyril and Methodius', but it will at last be essentially consistent linguistically and we will also be able to correct the work's title to 'Old Church Slavonic Mass'.

Weingart's doubly revised text in the 1930 vocal score can therefore be employed as our basic model. But Weingart's 1930 musical alterations should be standardised and his inappropriately jaunty dotted rhythms in bb. 5, 14, 30, 33 and 38 of the 'Slava' (see Example 3) should be changed to groups of crotchets. Likewise, his dactylic quaver and semiquaver rhythms in bb. 46, 56, 71, 80 and 89 of the 'Svet' should become three triplet quavers each time, as Weingart's vocal parts are unsingable at the speed marked. Večerka's emended forms 'chvaly', 'svet', 'krštenije', 'otpuštenije', 'za ny', 'zeml'a' and 'vsa' should be incorporated. Seven more modifications not affecting the syllable count should also be carried out. Janáček's 'Sabaoth' (Table 1, line 54) – his own invention in accordance with Latin orthography – should be changed to 'Sabaot' (OCS 'Sabaotъ'). The composer's 'jimže' (Table 1, line 29), derived from modern Czech spelling, ought to be OCS 'imže'. Another vital change is the alteration of Janáček's meaningless 'natvych' in b. 368 of the 'Věruju' to the correct word 'mrtvych' (Table 1, line 52). The other four emendations not altering the syllable count all concern double consonants: in 'istinna', 'istinnago'

Slava, bb. 69–70

Věruju, b. 87

Věruju, bb. 287–8

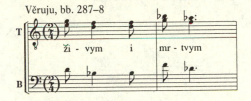

Věruju, bb. 323–4

Svet, b. 105 (similarly bb. 122 and 128–30)

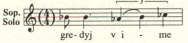

Svet, b. 111 (similarly b. 116)

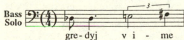

Ex. 4a

41

Svet, bb. 45–6 (similarly bb. 55–6, 70–1, 79–80 and 88–9)

pl - na sut ne - be - sa i ze - ml'a sla - vy tvo - je - je.

Ex. 4b

Věruju, b. 11

v je - di - no - go Bo - ga,

Ex. 4c

and 'Osanna' twice (Table 1, lines 27, 56 and 58). There are no double consonants in OCS. Vajs's 'istinna' and 'istinnago' are the results of the removal of weak jers from 'istinьna' and 'istinьnago', but when dropping the jer each time he should have also omitted an 'n'. The word 'Hosanna' is of course foreign to OCS; most manuscripts adapt it in line with OCS orthography to 'Osana'.

All the final revisions outlined so far require no musical changes, but all bar one of the remaining necessary ones require tiny adjustments to Janáček's vocal lines. The three surviving vocalisations of weak jers in 'vozdajem', 'voplti' and 'vo ime' should be corrected (as Weingart suggested in 1928), producing the following forms: 'vzdajem', 'vplti' and 'v ime' (Table 1, lines 8, 33 and 57). The words 'voskrse' and 'voskrsenija' should not be emended, however, despite Weingart's assertion that they ought to be (see p. 36). In place of 'živym, mrtvym' and 'životvoreštago' there should be the correct forms 'živym i mrtvym' and 'životvoreštago'. The negligible musical tinkering required to add all these corrections is shown in Example 4a. The proper form of the second line of the 'Svet', 'plna sut nebesa i zeml'a slavy tvojeje' can be included with little more recomposition – see Example 4b. Finally, in b. 11 of the 'Věruju' the words 'v je-di-no-go' are allotted only three notes, so a small musical change is required (Example 4c).

The syllabification, capitalisation and punctuation in the printed version of the Mass are modern and haphazard. Restoring OCS syllabification is easy: all syllables bar final ones must end in a vowel (Gardiner 1984, 24). But attempting to reinstate OCS punctuation would be absurd. In OCS manuscripts, suspended dots often separate groups of words and larger units are sometimes detached by collections of dots or of dots and lines, but these markings are inconsistent. Moreover, there is no capitalisation in OCS; individual words are not even distinguished. Standardised modern punctuation and ecclesiastical capitalisation can therefore be applied for the sake of clarity.

There are three remaining insoluble problems. First, in bb. 28–30, 31–3 and 36–8 of the 'Slava' the word 'člověkom' is left out (it is included in bb. 3–5 and 9–14). Although these omissions are unfortune, adding the missing word in all three instances would distort Janáček's musical motives. Second, we could not reinstate the four whole phrases of text left out accidentally by Janáček without rewriting the music to an unacceptable extent. Last of all, Janáček sets the text largely with anachronistic modern Czech first-syllable accentuation throughout the entire Mass, despite the fact that OCS almost certainly had movable stress. Rectifying this would be impossible for two reasons. First, we would have to recompose the work completely. And second, we would not know exactly what to replace Janáček's stress patterns with: precise details of OCS accentuation cannot be ascertained and imitating the stress patterns of modern CS would also be anachronistic.

Table 1 thus shows the conglomerate Weingart (1930)/Večerka/ Wingfield text. Square brackets denote text not used by Janáček in the final version of the work and round ones show textual repetitions occurring out of sequence.

Table 1

Line	Movement	Church Slavonic	English
1	Gospodi	Gospodi, pomiluj. Chrste, pomiluj. Gospodi, pomiluj.	Lord, have mercy. Christ, have mercy. Lord, have mercy.
	Slava	Slava vo vyšn'ich Bogu i na zeml'i mir, člověkom blagovol'enija. Chvalim te, blasgoslovl'ajem te, klan'ajem ti se, siavoslovim te, chvaly vzdajem tebě velikyje radi slavy tvojeje, [Gospodi Bože, Cěsarju nebeskyj,] Bože Otče Vsemogyi.	Glory to God in the highest and in earth peace, good will towards men. We praise thee, we bless thee, we worship thee, we glorify thee, we give thanks to thee for thy great glory, [O Lord God, heavenly King,] God the Father Almighty.
10		Gospodi, Synu jedinorodnyi, Isuse Chrste; Gospodi Bože, Agneče Božii, Synu Oteč, vzeml'ej grěchy mira, pomiluj nas. [Vezeml'ej grěchy mira,] primi mol'enija naša. Sědej o desnuju Otca, pomiluj nas. Jako ty jedin svet; ty jedin Gospod; ty jedin vyšn'ij, Isuse Chrste so Svetym Duchom, vo slavě Boga Otca. Amin.	O Lord, the only-begotten Son, Jesu Christ; O Lord God, Lamb of God, Son of the Father, that takest away the sins of the world, have mercy upon us. [Thou that takest away the sins of the world,] receive our prayer. Thou that sittest at the right hand of the Father, have mercy upon us. For thou only art holy; thou only art the Lord; thou only art most high, O Jesu Christ with the Holy Ghost, in the glory of God the Father. Amen.
20	Věruju	Věruju v jedinogo Boga, Otca Vsemoguštago, Tvorca nebu i zeml'i, vidimym vsěm i nevidimym. (Amin.) Věruju i v jedinogo Gospoda Isusa Chrsta, Syna Božija jedinorodnago, i ot Otca roždenago prěžde vsěch věk, Boga ot Boga, Svět ot Světa, Boga istina ot Boga istinago, roždena, ne stvor'ena, jedinosuštna Otcu, imže vsa byše;	I believe in one God, the Father Almighty, Maker of heaven and earth, of all things visible and invisible. (Amen.) And (I believe) in one Lord Jesus Christ, the only-begotten Son of God, and begotten of his Father before all worlds, God of God, Light of Light, very God of very God, begotten, not made, being of one substance with the Father, by whom all things were made;

who for us men
and for our salvation came down from heaven,
and was incarnate by the Holy Ghost of the Virgin Mary,
[and was made man,] (I believe.)
and was crucified also for us [under Pontius Pilate],
he suffered and was buried;
and on the third day he rose again according to the Scriptures,
and ascended into heaven,
and sitteth on the right hand of the Father;
and he shall come again
with glory to judge the quick and the dead;
and his kingdom shall have no end.
  And (I believe) in the Holy Ghost,
The Lord and giver of life,
who proceedeth from the Father and the Son,
who with the Father and the Son together
is worshipped and glorified,
who spake by the Prophets;
and in one Holy, Catholic
and Apostolic Church;
and I acknowledge one baptism
for the remission of sins;
and I look for the resurrection of the dead
and the life of the world to come. Amen.

Holy, holy, holy, Lord God of Hosts,
heaven and earth are full of thy glory.
[Hosanna in the highest.]
Blessed is he that cometh in the name of the Lord.
Hosanna in the highest.

O Lamb of God, [that takest away the sins of the world,] have
    mercy upon us.
O Lamb of God, that takest away the sins of the world, [have
    mercy upon us.]
O Lamb of God, [that takest away the sins of the world, grant us
    thy peace.] have mercy upon us.

30

iže nas radi člověk
i radi našego spasenija snide s nebes,
i vplti se ot Ducha Sveta iz Marije Děvy,
[i včlověči se,] (věruju,)
raspet že za ny [pri Pontiscěm Pilatě],
mučen i pogreben byst;
i voskrse v tretij den po Pisaniju,
i vzide na nebo,
sědit o desnuju Otca;
i paky imat priti

40

sudit živym i mrtvym so slavoju;
jegože česarstviju nebudet konca.
  (Věruju) i v Ducha Svetago,
Gospoda i životvoreštago,
ot Otca i Syna ischodeštago,
s Orcem že i Synom kupno
poklan'ajema i soslavima,
iže glagolal jest Proroky;
i jedinu Svetuju, Katoličesku
i Apostolsku Crkov;

50

i spovědaju jedino krštenije
v otpuštenije grěchov;
i čaju voskrsenija mrtvych
i života buduštago věka. Amin.

Svet   Svet, svet, svet, Gospod Bog Sabaot,
plna sut nebesa i zeml'a slavy tvojeje.
[Osana vo vyšn'ich.]
Blagoslovl'en gredyj v ime Gospodn'e.
Osana vo vyšn ich.

Agneče   Agneče Božij, [vzeml'ej grěchy mira,] pomiluj nas.

60

Agneče Božij, vzeml'ej grěchy mira, [pomiluj nas.]

Agneče Božij, [vzeml'ej grěchy mira, daruj nam mir,] pomiluj
    nas.

Approximate OCS pronunciation guide for English speakers

a, e, o	as in 'map', 'red', 'not'
i	'ee' in 'meet'
u	'oo' in 'good', but more rounded
y	shorter than 'i'; approximately as in 'heavy'
ě	'ye' in 'yet'
j, ja, je	'y', 'ya', 'ye' in 'yet', 'yak', 'yes'
c	'ts' in 'bits' (sounded together)
č	'ch' in 'church'
b, d, k, p, t	as in English, but not aspirated
g	hard, as in 'gold', but not aspirated
ch	approximately as in Scottish 'loch'
l, m, n, v	as in English
r	pronounced with a single flap of the tongue against the gums behind the upper teeth
s	as in 'see'
š	'sh' in show
z	as in 'zip'
ž	's' in 'pleasure'
l', n', r'	These palatal consonants are modified by the placing of the middle part of the back of the tongue against the hard palate during their articulation. They may be pronounced as 'ly', 'ny' (e.g. as in 'canyon') and 'ry', but with the two sounds enunciated as close together as possible
št, žd	The two consonants in each of these combinations should also be sounded as close together as possible

3

The authentic score

Introduction

Recent Janáček research has revealed that many published editions of the composer's music contain alterations that he did not initiate and that he either sanctioned only reluctantly or never authorised.[1] Granted this tradition of external interference in Janáček's works, it is scarcely surprising that the authenticity of the published version of the *Glagolitic Mass* is questionable. The printed text is problematic in three respects: it contains several drastic late-1927 alterations that were apparently forced on the composer; the order of the movements in all editions of the Mass is different from that used in the two performances in Janáček's lifetime; and in all printed full scores an offstage instruction applying to the clarinet parts in the 'Věruju' has been suppressed. This chapter questions the validity of those changes. A detailed description of them is followed by an evaluation of why they were made. Their musical consequences are then examined. Finally, guidelines for future performances and editions of the Mass are offered.

Survey of the important late-1927, 1928 and 1929 revisions

Many of the last-minute 1927 emendations outlined on p. 13 – e.g. doublings of existing lines – were small-scale and can be shown to have been devised by Janáček (see Blážek 1969, 684; and Wingfield 1987b, 189–201). But five major, much more dubious alterations were made in the Mass in November 1927: one each in the 'Úvod', 'Gospodi' and 'Svet', and two in the 'Věruju'. The first of these to be effected was the simplification of the rhythmic organisation of the 'Úvod'. This movement is constructed from three motives, the second of which is a rhythmic transformation of the first. These motives are marked 'd', 'e' and 'f' in Example 5, which contains the original version of bb. 1–6. All three motives are notated

throughout the printed 'Úvod' in 3/4. The original version of the movement, on the other hand, has a bolder rhythmic design. Here motive 'e' is
notated in 5/8 as seven quavers to be played in the time of five, whereas in
the printed text it takes the form of four quavers followed by three triplet
quavers in 3/4. Also, 'f' is notated in 5/8 as opposed to 3/4 and its second
bar consists of five quavers rather than a crotchet and four quavers.
Throughout the original version there is a dual time-signature and each
motive operates on its own rhythmic plane, producing a metrical conflict
based on the digits 3, 5, and 7 (members of the prime number series).

Ex. 5

Ex. 5 *continued*

49

The important late-1927 alteration in the 'Gospodi' is also a rhythmic simplification, made shortly after the rhythmic reorganisation of the 'Úvod'. In Janáček's original version of the 'Gospodi', bb. 1–29, 76–8 and 85–90 have a 5/4 time-signature (the printed text has 4/4). Example 6 offers a transcription of the earlier version of the first seven bars of this movement. In the published score the main motive contains a mirror rhythm in its first bar, whereas the original form of this motive has an uneasy rhythmic asymmetry. Furthermore, the rapid descending figure first stated in b. 7 ('h' in Ex. 10, p. 67) is made up only of triplet quavers in

Ex. 6

Ex. 6 *continued*

the printed score, but it has a disconcerting fluctuation between duplets and triplets in the original version.

There are two very significant late-1927 revisions in the 'Věruju'. The first is the modification of the 'offstage' instruction applying to bb. 121–67 in the clarinets to 'offstage, if possible'. If these clarinet parts are not performed offstage, the character and orchestral balance of the passage is transformed completely. The second major alteration in the 'Věruju' is the

Ex. 7

most extensive 1927 change: the rewriting and substantial cutting of the 'Raspeť' section (bb. 210–48 of the published score). This passage was revised in the eight days before the premiere, after Jaroslav Kvapil had inserted two layers of conductor's markings into the Kulhánek score in red and brown pencils. The changes in the 'Raspeť' were so extensive that several pages had to be removed from the two authorised copies and new pages written by both Kulhánek and Sedláček had to be inserted. The orchestral parts also needed considerable modification. Essentially, the earlier version contains extra interjections played principally by three sets of pedal timpani between the organ solo phrases in bb. 210–31 of the printed text. The basic five-bar unit is shown in Example 7. This is stated beginning on triads of Db major (Example 7), D major, B minor and E minor respectively between bb. 209–10, 212–13, 215–16 and 230–1 of the Universal score. Then what are bb. 244–8 of the published score, which contain the same motive starting on a triad of Ab minor, have additional three-timpani rolls on oscillating chords of Ab minor in root position and E major in first inversion.

The last of the important revisions made in November 1927 is a fourteen-bar cut in the 'Svet', also made after Kvapil had inserted markings into his conductor's score. The discarded bars (shown in short score in Example 8) originally came between what are now bb. 182 and 183 of the published text. They develop two motives: an orchestral one stated initially in bb. 39–41 and a choral one that first appears in bb. 144–6.

Both the later (1928 and 1929) changes are omissions of written instructions. In the course of the 1927 rehearsals Janáček specified that the concluding Intrada should be played at the beginning of the work as well, which created a cyclical nine-movement structure with five choral movements framed by two orchestral introductions and two postludes. This arrangement is confirmed at the front of the conductor's (Kulhánek) score, although the relevant marking does not appear in the Sedláček score or the orchestral parts. Confusingly, the 1928 Kundera vocal score also omits the instruction, despite the fact that at the later April 1928 Prague perform-

Ex. 8

Ex. 8 *continued*

ance, attended by Janáček, the Intrada prefaced the work. Needless to say, the 1929 (posthumous) full score leaves out the marking too. Lastly, the 'offstage' marking in the 'Věruju', retained in the 1928 and 1930 vocal scores, was omitted from the 1929 orchestral score.

Reasons for the changes

The causes of the significant late-1927 alterations can be ascertained through analysis of four types of evidence: eye-witness accounts; the composer's correspondence; the manuscripts; and the music itself. Such an examination rapidly reveals that these emendations were forced on Janáček because of the lack of instrumental resources and the inadequacies of the performers who participated in the premiere. Firm evidence to support the theory that the rhythmic simplification of the 'Úvod' and 'Gospodi' was not initiated by Janáček is provided by the repetiteur for the 1927 vocal rehearsals, Vilém Blážek (1969, 684). He states that the metrical reorganisation of both movements was carried out because Kvapil and his forces found the original versions 'too difficult to manage'. This is not hard to believe as far as the 'Úvod' and bb. 7–9 of the 'Gospodi' are concerned. Cacophony would indeed have resulted in 1927 from a provincial orchestra weaned on Dvořák attempting to maintain a three-against-five-against-seven metrical conflict for seventy-seven bars. Furthermore, it can be appreciated why the perilously exposed alternating duplets and triplets (marked 'Presto') in the original version of bb. 7–9 of the 'Gospodi' might have created problems for such an orchestra. But both the orchestral and choral parts in bb. 1–6, 10–29 etc. of the 'Gospodi' seem innocuous to the modern eye. Nevertheless, the surviving chorus parts prove that the 5/4 time-signature did trouble the 1927 singers: these parts are full of pencil reminders about the fact that much of the movement is in 5/4, indicating that the 'Gospodi' was rehearsed more than once in its original form with several chorus members making repeated mistakes before Janáček was finally obliged to rewrite bb. 1–29, 76–8 and 85–90 in 4/4. Evidently, the technical proficiency of amateur choirs in Czechoslovakia was lower in 1927 than it is now.

Blážek does not outline any reasons for the important alterations in the 'Věruju'. Luckily, it is not difficult to discover why they were made from a brief examination of the music. The 'offstage' marking in b. 121 was obviously modified because in 1927 it was undeniably impractical. In the third movement of his *Symphonie fantastique* Berlioz allows enough time for an orchestral oboist both to leave his seat to play offstage and to return to the orchestra afterwards. But the three orchestral clarinettists in the *Glagolitic Mass* could not possibly perform the offstage passage, as they would have only one bar in which to go behind the scenes and as few as nine in which to return. In 1927 there were four possible solutions to this problem, none of them wholly satisfactory. First, three extra clarinettists could have been employed to wait offstage and play only this short section of the 'Věruju', an option that would have increased the expense and inconvenience of amassing an orchestra to perform the work. Second, the onstage clarinettists could have muted their instruments, e.g. by placing a leather bag over the bell, which would have been difficult to achieve in the short time available. Third, the onstage clarinet parts in bb. 94–119 and 177–8 could have been omitted, which would have allowed the three orchestral clarinettists time to adopt the offstage role. This solution would have necessitated the playing of the first clarinet's solos in bb. 100–4 and 108–12 by another wind instrument and would have resulted in the loss from bb. 96–100, 105–8 and 113–19 of the distinctive tone of the bass clarinet, an integral part of the main motive of the 'Věruju' (developed throughout bb. 94–119). Fourth, the clarinet parts in bb. 121–67 could have been played onstage. This would have meant sacrificing a striking orchestral effect. Kvapil and Janáček could not choose the first solution owing to lack of instrumental resources and in their haste they appear never to have considered the second and third ones. Thus for the premiere they were compelled to abandon the 'offstage' marking.

A slight problem with the original 'Raspet' section (equivalent to bb. 210–48 of the printed 'Věruju') is that it requires four percussionists (three timpanists and one more to play the side drum), whereas elsewhere in the Mass a maximum of three is needed. Kvapil may have objected to this. But the real difficulty is the actual music written for the three sets of timpani. When the first performance took place, the modern drum – equipped with a plastic head, tuning gauge and a central pedal with a ball-bearing clutch – did not exist. Indeed, machine timpani of any description were a novelty and many orchestras possessed only drums that had to be tuned manually. The Brno orchestra that played at the premiere did have a set of old-fashioned machine timpani, each with a calfskin head and fitted with a 'saw-tooth' clutch engaged by a side-action clutch liner and a master tuning handle. Tuning such instruments is a relatively slow, if reasonably accurate process; hence the quick retunings in Janáček's original 'Raspet' section, one to be achieved in as few as three bars, would have been impracticable. In addition, the original version of the passage requires a minimum of seven timpani; nine would be ideal, allowing every note to be sounded within the most effective part of the compass of at least one drum. As three drums are sufficient for the rest of the Mass (the modern complement of five would be better), and because the 1927 Brno orchestra possessed only one set of machine timpani, Janáček's initial 'Raspet' section was seen by the conductor to be unperformable. The composer was forced to abandon his ambitious orchestration and to omit the timpani phrases.

The reason for the deletion of fourteen bars from the 'Svet' is to be discovered in the extant manuscript parts for the choir. In the last two bars of the fourteen there are some very high chorus notes, particularly for the sopranos, who are asked to enter on bb^2, but also for the tenors, who are required to sing cb^2, and for the altos, who ascend to g^2. Pencil annotations, written in the chorus parts before the fourteen bars were cut, evidence the difficulties that the high notes caused the singers in rehearsal. These problems were so severe that an attempt was swiftly made to ease them. The soprano line was eliminated, the alto part transferred to the sopranos and the tenor line allotted to the altos. This temporary solution clearly proved troublesome, so Janáček had to omit the offending two bars. However, because that cut did not make sense musically, he was forced to leave out the preceding twelve bars as well. (Both the first of the fourteen deleted bars and b. 183 of the printed version begin on a C major chord, so at least the more extensive cut maintains a sense of continuity.)

The cause of the 1928 omission of the instruction concerning the Intrada is more difficult to evaluate. Kundera used the Sedláček copy as his exemplar for the 1928 vocal score. As the marking in question occurs only in the conductor's (Kulhánek) copy, its omission from the 1928 print could have been an oversight. This is unlikely, however, since Kundera actually specifies the nine-movement form in his February 1928 analysis of the Mass (p. 189): 'The work has a double instrumental introduction and a double instrumental postlude.' Another possibility is that Janáček asked Kundera to leave out the instruction, but this is equally improbable, because the vocal score was published before the April 1928 performance in Prague of the nine-movement version.

Only if we view the problem as a performance practice issue does a potential solution emerge. Kundera remarks: 'According to an old custom . . . festal masses were begun and concluded by intradas.' (1928, 189). Indeed, exuberant intradas with trumpets and drums were a vital part of Czech masses on feast days from as early as the first half of the eighteenth century. Janáček was fully acquainted with this tradition. In his article 'Without Drums', published in *Lidové noviny* on 16 April 1911, he describes taking part when he was seven in a raid from Hukvaldy to a neighbouring village to 'borrow' a set of drums, the prospect of not having any for the festal mass the next day being regarded as unthinkable. Kvapil and his 1927–8 performers were all presumably as aware of the custom as Janáček, because it was considered necessary only to write a brief instruction in the conductor's score and nothing in the (surviving) parts used for the Brno and Prague performances. Thus Kundera may not have deemed it vital to include the marking in his vocal score, which after all was intended largely for rehearsing the voice parts; Czech conductors would presumably adopt the nine-movement form automatically. Of course, Janáček died before the full score was issued and the editorial staff of Universal Edition simply followed the eight-movement structure of the Sedláček score. Had they used the Kulhánek copy instead as an exemplar, they would certainly have either printed the relevant marking at the beginning of their edition or placed the Intrada first and added an instruction to repeat this movement after the Organ Solo.

The omission of the 'offstage' instruction from the 'Věruju' in the full score is a clear-cut case of editorial interference. Janáček cannot have authorised the 1929 blue-pencil deletion of this in the Sedláček score, as he was dead. A Universal editor clearly felt that the indecisive modified form of the marking ('offstage, if possible') justified his leaving it out altogether.

A general picture of the external practical considerations governing the major revisions from late 1927 to 1929 has now emerged. The drastic nature of some of the 1927 changes still remains to be explained; problematic passages were mutilated or removed completely. To discover the reasons for this an examination of the circumstances surrounding both performances in Janáček's lifetime is required. Immediately striking is the fact that there were too few rehearsals involving the orchestra for the invention of sophisticated solutions to the difficulties concerning the instrumentalists. There were only four orchestral rehearsals for the Brno premiere and two for the Prague concert. Both orchestras had their work cut out merely to learn their parts: Kaprál's 1928 review mentions that the Brno orchestra was under-rehearsed (see p. 120). Also, since Janáček did not attend a rehearsal for the premiere until 18 November (Blážek 1969, 684), he had only a little more than two weeks in which to make the revisions and to have substantial emendations made in both authorised copies and the parts.

Another important factor is that throughout the entire period in which the rehearsals for the first performance took place, Janáček was preoccupied with *From the House of the Dead*. On 30 November, after the full practices for the *Glagolitic Mass* had started, the composer wrote to Kamila: 'I am finishing one work after another – as if I had to account for my life . . . With the new opera I am hurrying like a baker throwing loaves into the oven.' (Štědroň 1953, 615). Janáček next wrote to Kamila about the opera on 2 December, only three days before the premiere of the Mass: 'I am finishing perhaps my greatest work – this latest opera. I feel so excited, as if my blood wanted to gush out'.[2] Evidently, one of the composer's most intense periods of work on his last opera took place while the rehearsals for the first performance of the Mass were happening, further reducing the time available for him to resolve the practical difficulties uncovered by these rehearsals.

Musical considerations

A comparison of the original and the published (1929) full scores of the Mass show that the late major revisions have marred the structure of the work, lessened its dramatic impact, suppressed some of its most innovatory features and obscured the influence of other contemporary composers on Janáček. First, the original 'Úvod' embodies a much more powerful build-up of tension than does its foursquare published counterpart. Throughout the earlier version there is a conflict not only between metres, but also between two motives, one of which is defined rhythmically and the other of which is not ('d' and 'e' in Example 5). Both these dynamic rhythmic conflicts were lost when the metre of the movement was standardised.

The simplification of the 'Úvod' has also distorted our perception of the influences on Janáček's late style. During the twenties the composer was at last exposed to a substantial quantity of contemporary European music. In early September 1925 he attended the ISCM Festival in Venice, where he heard a variety of recent chamber works (see Haefeli 1982, 483–4, for details of what was played). One of these pieces was Hindemith's *Kammermusik 2* for piano and twelve solo instruments (1924), which employs 3/8 and 4/4 time-signatures simultaneously in the third movement. *Kammermusik 2* certainly seems to have influenced the scoring, harmony and form of Janáček's late chamber works. Moreover, the composer's pre-1925 music contains no similar rhythmic complexities. Thus, although Hindemith's metrical experimentation appears unadventurous in comparison with that of Ives or even with that of Berlioz in *Les Troyens*, it was probably the catalyst for Janáček's use of a dual time-signature in the 'Úvod' of the *Glagolitic Mass*.

Equally detrimental are the rhythmic changes in the 'Gospodi', which have, for example, affected adversely the relationship between words and music. In his November 1927 article (pp. 116–19) Janáček describes the principal motive of the 'Gospodi' ('g') as the 'motive of a desperate frame of mind'. However, the rhythm of the printed (4/4) form of this motive does not convey desperation at all. The unsettling alternation between two- and three-crotchet groupings in the earlier version is much more anguished.

The musical consequences of the two major revisions in the 'Věruju' are particularly unfortunate. Bb. 121–67 of the original 'Věruju' contain a magical piece of orchestration. These bars form the beginning of an orchestral commentary on the crucifixion. The mystic atmosphere of this section is lost if offstage clarinets are not employed. Moreover, if onstage instruments are used, the extent of Janáček's exploration of orchestral effects in the last five years of his life is obscured. In *The Makropulos Affair* enterprising use is made of an offstage brass ensemble; the Sinfonietta exploits the contrasting sonorities of a brass band and a symphony orchestra before integrating the two at the end of the finale. The orchestration in bb. 121–67 of the 'Věruju' of the *Glagolitic Mass* constitutes the culmination of Janáček's spatial experimentation in his late works. Indeed the texture here is similar to that of Ives's *The Unanswered Question* (1906), in which the onstage instruments carry on a dialogue to the impassive accompaniment of the offstage group.

Janáček's version of the 'Raspet' employing the three sets of timpani is preferable to the simplified one for several reasons. To start with, the late-1927 emendations have created structural problems in the movement. In bb. 244–8 of the printed score three piccolos, the brass and the timpani have an isolated statement of a five-bar motive that is not employed elsewhere in the 'Věruju'. Janáček's use of material in the Mass is extremely economical, so this under-used motive is anomalous. Naturally, deviations from a norm are important events in some of Janáček's compositions. But the proportions of the 'Věruju' seem to demand more expansive treatment of the three-piccolo, brass and timpani motive. A vast, controlled build-up takes place in bb. 120–209, culminating in a high region in bb. 210–48, which constitute the structural peak of the whole work.[3] In the printed score the high region is too abrupt to be a suitable outlet for the enormous amount of tension accumulated in bb. 120–209; only the longer original version of the section (which incorporates four extra statements of the motive in bb. 244–8 of the published score) is substantial and dramatic enough to perform this function.

A further problem is that the published version of the 'Raspet' contains nonsensical speed markings. In b. 210 we find 'Allegro', which becomes

'Presto' in b. 216. There is no new tempo marking in b. 231, where the time-signature changes from 6/4 to 2/4, but Janáček's triplet markings in bb. 231–45 indicate a proportional relationship of dotted minim = minim. Apparently, the chorus is expected to articulate the text of the 'Raspet' at the impossible speed of minim = c. 144! Vogel, who conducted the work in Brno in 1958, was so troubled by this section in the final version that he felt obliged to remark: 'It is recommended that instead of preceding the Crucifixus with a hesitant *ritardando* conductors should take the 2/4 section [bb. 231–48] . . . at half the speed so as . . . to give the passage the massive weight it needs.' (1963, 322). Janáček's version incorporating the timpani statements is, however, yet more logical. The organ phrases in what are now bb. 210–30 are marked 'Allegro' then 'Presto', as in the printed score, each of the subsequently deleted timpani interjections bearing the indication 'Tempo I' – i.e. 'Con moto (crotchet = 100)'. The organ and vocal phrases in the equivalent of bb. 231–43 of the published score also have the clear indication 'Tempo I', 'Maestoso' succeeding this marking in b. 244. Thus Vogel's instinct was correct; but what are now bb. 231–48 in the printed score should be performed even more slowly than he supposed. The hasty late-1927 alterations have rendered the 'Raspet' utterly incoherent. Luckily, all the structural and tempo problems can be solved simply by restoring Janáček's original timpani interjections.

Another consequence of the late-1927 rewriting of the 'Raspet' is that it has reduced the impact of the climax of the whole Mass. The 'Raspet' clearly had a special significance for Janáček from an early stage, as he wrote an overtly programmatic remark next to the main organ motive of the section in his first draft of the 'Věruju': 'the expulsion of the degenerate traders from the temple'.[4] This insertion, a rare programmatic insight afforded by Janáček's manuscripts, indicates that the composer viewed his orchestral commentary on the crucifixion at least partly as a summary of Jesus's life and that he saw Jesus's violent expulsion of the money-lenders to be associated symbolically with the crucifixion. The connection of these two events is presumably inspired by Matthew's Gospel, where the ejection by Jesus of the corrupt money-lenders from the temple presages the purging shortly after the crucifixion of this house of worship through the rending of its veil, a symbol of the corrupt practices of the Pharisees. Janáček appears to have decided as early as his first draft to eschew the customary anguished, sorrowful mode of setting the 'Crucifixus' and to concentrate instead on that section's violent programmatic aspects, making it into an explosive and dramatic musical peak. All the composer's subsequent 1926 revisions of the 'Raspet' served to strengthen its function as the focal point of the whole Mass. In his own (1927) words (see p. 119 below): 'I am representing . . . the heavens being torn open when Christ was crucified on the cross . . . I depict thunder and flashes of lightning.' (he wrote these comments to Kamila before the timpani phrases were removed). Unfortunately, the late-1927 alterations removed the thunderous timpani interjections and muted the impact of one of the most powerful and exciting passages of music that Janáček ever wrote.

Also obscured by the November 1927 revisions is Janáček's status as a pioneer in the history of orchestration. Having been invented in the nineteenth century, machine timpani were largely ignored by composers until the beginning of the twentieth. The earliest clear-cut uses of these instruments can be found in D'Indy's *Jour d'été à la montagne* (1905) and Strauss's *Salome* (first performed in 1905). Stravinsky employs two timpanists (sometimes playing chords) in *Le sacre* (1913) and Nielsen experiments with timpani glissandi in his Fourth Symphony (1916). But Janáček's thematic and harmonic use of three sets of pedal timpani throughout a substantial section of a movement is certainly novel.[5]

Janáček's idea of writing for more than one set of machine drums can be traced to Nielsen. In 1921 Brod sent Janáček a score of Nielsen's Fourth Symphony, which has virtuoso parts for two timpanists. On 11 June of the same year Janáček wrote to Brod: 'On your recommendation I have looked through the score of Nielsen's Symphony "The Inextinguishable". I will not criticise the work, because one finds in every piece something on which to build.' (Racek and Rektorys 1953, 79). These comments are characteristically laconic and scarcely wildly enthusiastic, but they do suggest that Nielsen's innovative orchestration influenced Janáček.

The November 1927 revision of the 'Věruju' may have undermined its peak, but the cut in the 'Svet' has all but removed the tonal turning-point of that movement. In Janáček's original version of the 'Svet' a conflict is set up in the opening 136 bars between three tonal centres: E, E♭ and D♭. This conflict is still unresolved at the beginning of the 'Osana', which starts on E♭. An E♭ pedal is held throughout bb. 137–78, then V of C major ensues in bb. 179–82. The remainder of the movement reconciles the earlier conflicting tonalities by interpreting D♭ as a flattened supertonic of C, and E and E♭ as the leading-note and flat seventh of F, the tonal goal of the movement. The closing tonal area is confirmed by a large-scale perfect cadence in bb. i–xiv and 183ff. Hence bb. 179–82 and i–x are the tonal turning-point of the movement, at last steering it towards F major. The removal of fourteen vital bars has rendered the key scheme virtually incomprehensible. (The tonal plan of this movement is examined in detail on p. 110.)

Numerous other formal problems have been created by this cut. For example, the awkward join between bb. 182 and 183 is made worse by the fact that the dynamic and registral peaks of the movement (both of which occur in bb. i–xiv) have been removed. Now the huge build-up in bb. 165–82 is followed immediately by an inexplicable drop in tension. It is impossible to make bb. 183–5 sound effective in performance, even if the strings and tenor are instructed to play and sing *fortissimo* in a vain attempt to compensate for the loss of the dynamic and registral highpoints.

All the changes examined so far have been detrimental to the Mass. That affecting the order of the movements is not serious. But performing the Intrada at both ends of the work is advantageous in some respects. The resulting nine-movement form has a satisfying symmetry: two pairs of instrumental movements frame five choral ones and the 'Věruju', the longest movement, is at the centre of the work. The cyclical return of the opening material also creates a connection between the Mass and three other late Janáček compositions – the First String Quartet, *Youth* and the Sinfonietta.

Guidelines for future editions and performances

In summary, the major late-1927 and 1929 changes constitute an un-satisfactory compromise that was imposed on Janáček and the 1928 removal of the opening Intrada was most probably not authorised by him. We are now in a position to assess whether the practical difficulties encountered in 1927 are still problematic today and to propose guidelines for future performances of the Mass.

First of all, the rhythmic simplification of the 'Gospodi' is no longer necessary: a modern choir will have minimal difficulty with Janáček's 5/4 phrases and a brief rehearsal will enable one of today's orchestras to master the original version of bb. 7–9. The 'Úvod' is more problematic. Since the original three rhythmic planes require the conductor to beat a very slow bar = 24 at the present metronome marking (crotchet = 72), individual players might easily lose all sense of pulse. Fortunately, Janáček appears to have anticipated this difficulty, because his metronome marking before he simplified the 'Úvod' was a quicker bar = 44. This speed could be re-instated, although the original version of the movement will still need careful preparation.

The offstage clarinets in the 'Věruju' are now a much less difficult proposition. Most modern orchestras could call on the services of three extra clarinettists; the part for the offstage instruments could even be taped for use in a live performance if absolutely necessary. Naturally, the offstage effect is straightforward to simulate in a recording studio, as is demonstrated by the 1984 Mackerras recording. Given the impressive technical standards achieved by modern choirs, the restoration of the fourteen bars missing from the 'Svet' is also reasonably unproblematic: the singers on the 1984 Mackerras recording sound only a little strained on the high notes. Besides, if a choir were unable to manage this passage, an alternative to cutting the fourteen bars does exist. Some of the altos could double the tenors, the remaining altos could be reinforced by those sopranos unable to produce a convincing *bb2*, and the rest of the sopranos could be doubled by appropriate orchestral instruments not employed here (e.g. clarinets 1 and 2 and the violins). To rescore these bars is preferable to removing them altogether.

Slightly more troublesome is the 'Raspet' section. Admittedly, the drums themselves are no longer a problem: most orchestras will be able to amass at least seven pedal timpani. Also, though the technical difficulty of the timpani parts is high, so is that of such standard repertoire works as Bartók's Concerto for Orchestra. In fact, even the passage quoted in Example 9 – from bb. 83–6 of the 'Slava' of the *Glagolitic Mass* – is just as difficult. Furthermore, a reduction of the number of retunings required in

Ex. 9

the 'Raspet' could be achieved through rearrangement of the part-writing. There is a minor problem concerning the reconstruction of Janáček's 'ideal' version of the section. After he omitted the timpani interjections he made some small musical changes: e.g. the odd accidental in the organ part was altered and the final Ab minor outburst (bb. 244–8 of the printed score) was pruned slightly. Thus it appears that we should not restore the original version of the passage, but rather we should insert the four deleted phrases into the published version. Finally, in an emergency an orchestra unable to find enough drums could employ brass instruments to play any missing notes. This solution should be regarded as a last resort, because the actual orchestration of the section is its most important single element.

Future editions of the Mass should reinstate the fourteen bars lost from the 'Svet', the 'offstage' instruction in the 'Věruju' and the 5/4 rhythms in the 'Gospodi'. Alternative versions of the relatively short 'Úvod' could be printed. The phrases involving the three sets of timpani should be added to the main text of the 'Raspet' and the Intrada ought to be printed first with an instruction to repeat the movement after the Organ Solo. A preface could explain the two possible arrangements of the Mass and point out that in the unlikely event of a liturgical performance the nine-movement form should definitely be performed. Such a layout for a new edition would fulfil both scholarly and practical needs without significantly increasing the amount of printed material. It would give a conductor the choice of performing either version. The two could even be mixed, for example if a group of performers wanted to present the original version but could not manage the rhythmically complex form of the 'Úvod'. But the whole of the original score ought to be played wherever possible. Only when we make a greater effort to understand Janáček's intentions will we be able to appreciate fully the work's stunning originality.

4

Synopsis

Intrada

The Mass begins with a festive orchestral Intrada, which would accompany the entry of the clergy in a liturgical performance.[1] This short movement is overtly secular in style. There are two sharply contrasting main motives: 'a' (bb. 1–2), in the strings and wind, is bustling, syncopated and chromatic; 'b' (bb. 4–6), a joyous brass fanfare, is sonorous, rhythmically regular and diatonic.[2] (All the work's main motives are quoted with their designated labels in Example 10.) Each time 'b' appears it is heard in conjunction with repetitions of a pounding dactylic motive ('c' – introduced by the timpani in b. 3), and its final note is decorated by a truncated variant ('b1') in the trumpets. In bb. 1–24 the two principal motives are varied in alternating blocks, brief repetitions of the opening of motive 'a' punctuating the 'b' blocks, all except the third (bb. 17–19) of which incorporate two statements of the brass fanfare. A structural *accelerando* is effected here by the compression of both blocks: 'a' shrinks from two bars to one; 'b' reduces gradually, from eighteen through ten and nine to eight minim beats. In bb. 25–32 brass and timpani reiterations of 'c' play a subsidiary role to five consecutive and rapidly diminishing 'b' blocks, which span four, four, three, three and two minims respectively. Next, bb. 33–5 combine motives 'b' and 'c' for the first time; then 'a', 'b' and 'c' all collide in an exuberant Ab major cadential passage, the final three minim units of which are separated emphatically by semibreve silences.

Úvod

After the Intrada comes another secular-sounding, purely instrumental movement: the 'Úvod' (the Introduction proper). This is abrasive and energetic. The opening grand, imitative brass and timpani fanfare ('d') is interrupted as early as b. 5 by two metrically contrasting motives, one ('e') a

Ex. 10

Ex. 10 *continued*

Ex. 10 *continued*

Ex. 10 *continued*

Ex. 10 *continued*

complete transformation of the intervallic content of the fanfare, and the other ('f') a close derivative of 'd'. These motives initiate a three-against-five-against-seven metrical conflict that persists until the final bar. Superficially, the form of the 'Úvod' is a loose rondo, governed by returns of the fanfare: *ABA'B'CA''* (bb. 1–17, 18–30, 31–3, 34–48, 49–63 and 64–77).

Much of the movement's impetus derives from the continual juxtaposition, superimposition and overlapping of its metrically conflicting motives, within a kaleidoscope of shifting dominant-, major- and minor-seventh harmonies.

Janáček's treatment of motive 'f' also creates a drive through to the closing bars, because, whereas 'd' and 'e' remain essentially unaltered other than by transposition, 'f' is constantly modified. At least five variants of 'f' can be identified (bb. 20–1, 24–6, 45, 49–63 and 72–5). Having been compressed to a single bar in b. 45, it is expanded to a vast melodic arc spanning fully fifteen bars (bb. 49–63) and is then transformed into a cadential figure. The continual alteration of 'f' underlines the progressive tonal plan, which reveals its goal (E) as late as b. 64. At the start, leading-note tendencies are avoided by means of modal inflections: an Aeolian configuration on Eb is followed by a Mixolydian one on Gb, and so on. The central part of the 'Úvod' passes swiftly through several disparate key areas, further evading any strong tonal implications. In b. 62 Gb returns, heralding the harmonic turning-point in bb. 64–9, where an enharmonic dominant seventh of B is superimposed on I of E, the first such clash in the movement. This event is highlighted by the first use of full orchestra in the 'Úvod' and by incisive timpani acciaccatura demisemi-quavers (added to bb. 66–9 by Janáček in late 1927). The tension is resolved in bb. 70–7 by a powerful consolidation of E major.

Gospodi pomiluj

The 'Gospodi' (Kyrie) adheres fundamentally to the customary *ABA'* arrangement with a separate section for each line of text (bb. 1–36, 37–75 and 76–90), although a textual overlap occurs as the result of the prema-ture return of the words 'Lord have mercy' in b. 68. The initial *A* section is itself tripartite: bb. 1–15, 16–25 and 26–36. Subsection *Ai* is a fifteen-bar instrumental introduction, which brings in two motives. Bb. 1–3 contain what Janáček describes in his November 1927 article (p. 116) as 'the motive of a desperate frame of mind' ('g'), which is transposed immediately in bb. 4–6. Each of the two halves of this motive reproduces part of the contour of the opening fanfare of the 'Úvod', but the intervals are nar-rowed, outlining dissonant diminished- and half-diminished seventh[3] har-monies. Motive 'g' creates a tense atmosphere, as a result of its tonal ambiguity, 5/4 time-signature, sombre orchestration and accompanying

72

sforzando chords. Gloominess gives way to outright anguish in bb. 7–9, where a cascading, contorted 'Presto' motive ('h'), derived from the first three notes of 'g', plunges down despairingly through three octaves. The instrumental prelude is rounded off by two more statements of 'g', which is now joined by a cello variant of the cascading motive ('h1').

Subsection *Aii* starts in bb. 16–17 with a rhythmically compressed, less chromatic form of the 'motive of a desperate frame of mind' ('g1'). The opening choral utterance (bb. 18–20) is another variant ('g2'), integrating the rhythm of 'g' and the melodic outline of 'g1'. The hushed dynamic marking (*piano*) and the hanging second-inversion harmony imbue this plaintive, homophonic setting of 'Lord have mercy' with awed bewilderment. In bb. 21–5 'g1' and 'g2' are transposed; then 'g1' appears twice in the orchestra (bb. 26–9), its imitative treatment highlighting a temporary, uneasy resolution on to an E major triad. Section *A* concludes with a tonally unstable transitional *accelerando* to section *B*, whose arrival is anticipated by the unduly hasty appearance of a new rising four-note motive ('i') in bb. 29–36.

The already considerable tension accumulated in section *A* is now intensified in two principal stages: bb. 37–53 and 54–75. In subsection *Bi* the words 'Christ have mercy' are set thrice in the solo soprano to a motive ('j') that is closely related to 'g'. Each soprano utterance is preceded by, and coupled with, subsidiary instrumental repetitions of 'i'. There is also an unbroken accompanimental line in the violins. A sense of urgency is maintained in bb. 37–53 by various means: a faster tempo marking, tonal ambiguity, progressively shorter rests before each declaration of 'Christ have mercy' and a sustained *crescendo*. Bb. 51–3 vary the orchestral motive by surmounting it simultaneously with a free inversion.

Subsection *Bii* (bb. 54–75) swells to a *fortissimo*, anxiety-ridden highpoint in bb. 72–5. The heightening of tension is achieved not only through this *crescendo*, but by means of increased tonal instability and a proliferation of motivic activity. Three textural levels are now employed, the solo soprano and chorus (both of whom develop motive 'j') occupying the main two of these, and the orchestra (employing motive 'i') sustaining the third one. Five three-bar homophonic choral units provide the backbone of the subsection, the gaps between these units diminishing relentlessly. As the highpoint approaches (bb. 65–71) the soprano line becomes detached from the others, thereby creating overlaps and further complicating the texture. At the highpoint itself (bb. 72–5) a whole-tone hexachord on Gb is

73

reached and the fifth choral utterance is subsumed within a registrally highlighted, four-bar soprano variant of 'j' – the only vocal unit that is longer than three bars in the entire movement.

Bb. 76–90 are much more than a mildly emended recapitulation of *A*. Although partly a reprise of the 'Lord have mercy' material, this section is moulded by a process of motivic integration begun in b. 11 (where 'g' and 'h1' are combined). It is also overwhelmed by the impact of the highpoint in bb. 72–5. Motive 'g2' recurs in the chorus on I_4^6 of E in bb. 76–8. This motive is rendered more agitated by *forte* markings, a three-against-two rhythmic conflict, and the addition of orchestral *sforzando* chords, which were previously associated with motive 'i' in section *B*. There follows a full-scale *fortissimo* instrumental outburst of *B* material on bVI and V of E in bb. 79–84, which are equivalent to the orchestral parts of bb. 67–72 in motivic terms. The ascent of the violas to g^3 (!) in b. 83 imparts an element of anguished despair to this passage. The next three bars (85–7) summarise briefly the orchestral prelude (bb. 1–15), the cello motive ('g') appearing in a less contorted form and leading finally to an E major triad in root position. Only now is the stream of loud dynamic markings unleashed by the highpoint of bb. 72–5 quelled; the movement sinks to an exhausted *pianissimo* conclusion. A last chorus reiteration of 'g2' breaks off half-way through and is completed by the first oboe and violas. The nagging guilt in the concluding supplication 'Lord have mercy' is reflected through the replacement in the final bar of an expected E major triad by a whole-tone subset (E–G♯–A♯).

Slava

The 'Slava' has six sections arranged in a rondo pattern: *ABA'CC'A"* (bb. 1–38, 39–68, 69–86, 87–138, 139–80 and 181–228). On a higher level, the movement divides into two parts (bb. 1–86 and 87–228), which are separated by an emphatic break in continuity. Each part is underpinned by a large-scale harmonic progression to I of E/Fb major, and each culminates in a protracted structural peak (bb. 69–86 and 181–228). Janáček's deployment of the text differs slightly from the traditional arrangement. The standard Gloria text is bipartite according to meaning: God the Father is glorified, then God the Son is petitioned and extolled (Chapter 2, Table 1, lines 4–10 and 11–19). But it is customarily broken up for musical setting into eight subdivisions (lines 4–5, 6–7, 8, 9–12, 13–14, 15, 16–18 and 19), the fourth of which contradicts the overlying two-part structure. (These textual subdivisions are adhered to in Bach's B minor Mass and Beethoven's *Missa solemnis*, for example.) In contrast, Janáček creates only five subdivisions (lines 4–5, 6–7, 8, 10–14 and 15–19), using these as the basis for the first five musical sections of his 'Slava', and then repeating the last four lines of the fifth one in his concluding section. As a result, his principal musical division (between bb. 86 and 87) coincides almost exactly with the main textual one (there is an overlap of three words).

At start of the 'Slava' despondency is dispelled in a flash by the solo soprano's modally inflected 'joyous shout' (Janáček's description – see p. 116) and the airy, glistening orchestral combination of oboes, clarinet, carillon, harp and strings. Section *A* (bb. 1–38) contains five statements altogether of the initial portion of text glorifying God the Father (lines 4–5), three in the solo soprano and two in the chorus. After two introductory bars of ethereal harmonics and held notes in the violins and violas, the movement's naive principal motive ('k') enters in the first clarinet and undergoes immediate repetition (bb. 3–6). The soprano weaves her initial utterance ('k1') around the clarinet's pair of two-bar units. In bb. 7–8 the violin and viola introduction returns, then in bb. 9–23 'k' goes through several transpositions and minor intervallic variations, the soprano superimposing her second, more exalted 'joyous shout' ('k2') in bb. 9–14. This whole opening passage is accompanied by continuous reiterations of a simple arpeggio figure, which is first introduced in b. 3 and thereafter always supports motive 'k'.

In bb. 23–4 the untroubled progress of 'k' is suddenly brought to a halt. It is challenged briefly, then swept impatiently aside by a new one-bar instrumental motive, 'l', which is an elaboration of the latter half of the first bar of 'k'. Four bars of scurrying imitation follow, based on 'l' and its yet more concise variant, 'll' (bb. 24–7). In the remainder of the opening section (bb. 28–38), 'l' and 'll' play a subordinate role to three statements of motive 'm', which has the same basic outline as 'k'. When 'm' first appears (in the orchestra in bb. 28–30) it is embellished by the solo soprano's third declaration of the opening portion of text ('m1'). Next, it is modified ('m2') in a joint presentation by the chorus and orchestra (bb. 31–3), the horns and cellos twice echoing its closing interval. Finally, the chorus and orchestra (bb. 36–8) repeat it at a higher pitch.

At the start of section *B* (bb. 39–68) a substantial increase in tempo enhances the sense of urgency initiated by the abrupt entrance of motive 'l' in bb. 23–4. This entire section continues the incessant interplay between 'l' and its variant. After a passage formed exclusively from repetitions of these two units (bb. 39–56), the trombones introduce a new version of 'm' ('m3') in bb. 57–60. This overlaps with the first of two successive choral statements of a further variant ('m4') setting lines 6–7 of the text (beginning 'We praise thee'). A short orchestral link based on the last two notes of 'll' leads to the next section (*A'*), the preliminary focal point of the movement. This section, which returns to the opening tempo, maintains the loudest general dynamic level and the fullest orchestration to date. Its single choral utterance ('We give thanks to thee for thy great glory' in bb. 69–72) consists of a grandiose motive ('n' – related to 'm'), and an overlapping variant ('n1'). There follows an expansive orchestral development of two compressed variants of the new motive ('n2' and 'n3'), during the course of which 'n3' and the movement's principal motive ('k') are actually stated simultaneously (bb. 79–82). The section ends with three forceful descending statements of 'n3' (the last partly reiterated), which are underlined by the first entry of the timpani in the movement (bb. 83–6). Harmonically, part I closes on an F♭ major triad, which is rendered unstable not only by the preceding dominant preparation of E♭ major (bb. 78–82), but also by the inclusion of the root of this chord in a nearly-whole-tone hexachord on E♭ (E♭–F♭–G♭–A♭–B♭–C) spanning the bass line of bb. 83–7 (an oblique link between parts I and II).

There is a sudden, dramatic drop in tension in b. 87, which launches the movement's second, more powerful build-up. Section *C* (bb. 87–138) is unusually rich motivically, bringing in five new interrelated ideas: 'o', 'p', 'q', 'r' and 's'. The first of these – 'o', a plaintive thematic fragment stated in imitation – grows directly out of part I's concluding rising fifth. Motive 'o' overlaps with a spiky, whole-tone idea in the violins ('p'), and in b. 90 those two join forces to create the ostinato 'q', continuous reiterations of which provide the intervallic basis for the solo soprano's setting in bb. 90–6 of lines 10–11 of the text ('God the Father Almighty' etc.). A more positive mood is engendered in bb. 98–101, where the organ makes its inaugural appearance in the work by doubling the strings' sonorous interlocking-fifth idea, 'r' (which, like 'o', is imitative). From b. 98 to the end of b. 135 'r' and 'q' alternate; a modest increase in tension arises out of the frequent modification of, as well as the many overlaps between, the two motives. In this passage, 'q' supports vocal interjections, initially by the solo soprano (bb. 104–7 and 112–13) and later by the chorus (bb. 117–22, 126–8 and 130–5), which set lines 12–14 of the text (from 'O Lord God' to 'receive our prayer'). The soprano's utterances are all founded on the various transpositions of 'q', while the chorus fashions its apparently new plunging, imitative idea ('s') by compressing and reversing 'r'. In bb. 136–8 a transitional structural *ritardando* to the next, 'Maestoso' section (C') is effected by a decelerating rhythmic augmentation of 'q' in the orchestra.

Section C' (bb. 139–80), which maintains the overall *forte* dynamic level reached during section C, underlines the ever more clamorous praise lavished on God the Son in the closing subdivision of text (lines 15–19, but as yet not including 'Amen') by means of a gradated growth to a very high level of motivic and textural complexity. At the outset, a timpani figure introduces and then forms part of a compound motivic block (bb. 139–43), which is founded on the movement's second ascending majestic string and organ motive ('t'). This block also includes four woodwind statements of 'q' and consecutive two-bar utterances by the chorus basses and the solo tenor, who decorate the bass line of 't' and the instrumental repetitions of 'q' respectively. There are six progressively more complicated occurrences of this compound unit in bb. 140–80 (the last overlapping into b. 181), which embody a melodic ascent from bb^1 to g^3. The first 't' block (bb. 140–3), setting line 15, overlaps with a return of 'p', the spiky whole-tone motive (bb. 143–5). This six-bar process is then repeated at a higher pitch (bb. 146–51), after which a reiteration of 'p' engulfs the solo tenor's intervallically dependent intonation of the words 'For thou only art holy' (bb. 152–4). A return of the quadruplet ostinato 'q' (bb. 155–7) prefaces and overlaps with the third, longer and more complicated 't' block (bb. 157–61). This not only varies 'q' and adds an extra component – the plunging chorus motive 's' (first heard in bb. 117–19) – but also superimposes in the solo tenor and chorus basses two different lines of text, the first time that different words are sung simultaneously in the Mass.

The fourth 't' block (bb. 162–8) is again longer and more complex, as it now incorporates the whole-tone motive ('p'). A brief connecting passage based on the ostinato 'q' leads to the final two 't' blocks. So far each of these blocks has had a clear internal subdivision in the voice parts and some of the instrumental lines (the first one divides at b. 142 and so on). But in bb. 172–5 this subdivision is removed through overlapping of the block's constituent motivic units, a development that causes three phrases of text to be sung together in b. 173. The final five-bar 't' block (bb. 176–80), which extends the superimposition of three groups of words to two bars in bb. 178–9, is the apex of the process of textural intensification in section C', because there are overlaps in every bar between statements of its four motivic components.

The movement's second structural peak (bb. 181–228) is connected to the preceding build-up by an extension of motive 's' that straddles bb. 178–181. This passage surpasses the first focal point in length and sheer volume. The tension is kept up throughout it by the delaying of the arrival and consolidation of the movement's tonal goal (E) until bb. 197ff., and by the inexorable integration and condensation of the movement's major motives. To begin with, a faster tempo coincides with the arrival of I of Eb and the superimposition of part I and part II material in bb. 181–4: 's' is stated simultaneously with the opening 'Slava' motive 'k', which has already absorbed the quadruplet rhythm of the ostinato 'q'. The result of all this is the creation of a four-note motive ('u'), which combines elements of 'k' (from which it derives its pitches), 's' (which becomes its bass line) and 't' (whose contour it reverses). In bb. 190–7 an authentic cadence in E is prolonged by a repeat of the synthesis of part I and part II motives, a further tempo increase in b. 197 occurring in conjunction with the start of the solo tenor's fervent 'Amen' acclamations (set to motive 'u'). Thereafter the movement hurtles towards its close in exhilarating style. A 'Presto' duplet variant of the 'Amen' motive ('u1') is unveiled by the orchestra and four times reinforced by the chorus. Bb. 212–13 reintroduce at this much faster speed the variant of 'k' heard in bb. 181–2. This is superseded by two reiterated variants of 'u' ('u2' and 'u3'), which are punctuated by the final five choral 'Amens' (bb. 214–18). A less frantic tempo marking appears in b. 219 ('Allegro'), but the momentary lull of bb. 219–21 (employing 'u3') is disrupted immediately by an electrifying reduction by the timpani of the 'Amen' motive to a rhythmically accelerated version of its by now three-note bass part ('u4'), an event that is capped by this motive's compression to a single note in the concluding threefold acclamation of the tonic triad of E major.

Věruju

The text of the Creed consists of three parts, affirming belief in the Father, the Son and the Holy Ghost (lines 20–2, 23–41 and 42–53). The short first part is not usually broken up in musical settings, but the second and third normally have four and two subdivisions respectively, producing a total of seven smaller portions: lines 20–2, 23–31, 32–3, 34–5, 36–41, 42–9 and 50–3. Janáček also divides his 'Věruju' text into three main parts, adhering to the traditional format for his third (lines 42–53), but extending his first to the end of line 33 (beginning 'and was incarnate'), thereby detaching the passage referring to the crucifixion and resurrection (lines 34–41). In addition, he reorganises the text on the smaller scale to form nine, as opposed to the customary seven, subdivisions: lines 20–2, 23–5, 26–32, 33, 34–5, 36–40, 41, 42–7 and 48–53. Yet more significantly, he incorporates repetitions of 'I believe' in lines 23, 33 and 42, creating the potential for a rondo musical structure. (Janáček's first and third reiterations of this phrase of text follow the textual arrangement of the Credo of Beethoven's *Missa solemnis*.) As far as the music is concerned, the superficial formal plan is a sprawling rondo: *AA'BA''CDEFF'A'''* plus Coda (bb. 1–28, 29–45, 46–93, 94–119, 120–61, 162–209, 210–48, 249–88, 289–316, 317–41 and 342–99). Each section sets one subdivision of text, apart from *C* and *D*, which are purely instrumental. On a larger scale, there are three parts with a loose *ABA'* pattern (bb. 1–119, 120–316 and 317–99).

Janáček begins the 'Věruju' with a sprightly two-bar motive ('v'), which embodies 'steadfastness of faith and the swearing of allegiance', according to the composer (p. 117). However, even if the stereotyped unison presentation of this motive could be said to suggest confident belief, its musical content undoubtedly seems less optimistic: it is ambiguous tonally, and it has a restless accompanying trill and sombre instrumentation. After a modified repeat of 'v' (bb. 3–4), the last four notes are speeded up rhythmically to form a short, independent motive ('w'), which is developed in bb. 5–7. The first chorus utterance in bb. 8–10 ('x') supplants the usual joyous affirmation with a yearning, whole-tone setting of 'I believe', imparting a sense 'more of a *longing* for faith . . . than of the demonstrative swearing of an oath' (Vogel 1963, 320–1). In bb. 11–15 the remaining text devoted to the Father is sung by the chorus to an extended, harmonised variant of the opening 'allegiance' motive ('v'). Section *A* concludes with several chorus 'Amens', set to the four-note motive ('w') and embedded within an orchestral development of both 'v' and 'w'.

The strained atmosphere of the opening bars persists in section *A'* (bb. 29–45), at the beginning of which the despairing whole-tone choral 'I believe' makes a reappearance. The section continues with another tonally inconclusive passage (bb. 32–45) incorporating the following elements: frequent repetitions of 'w'; an interchange between modified tenor and solo bass statements of 'v' (setting lines 23–5 of the text); and various versions of two new instrumental motives – 'y' (an ascending and descending arpeggio figure simplifying the contour of 'v') and 'z' (derived from 'x'). By b. 45 a pervasive feeling of agonised doubt has been established.

In section *B*, lines 26–32 of the text are all allocated to the solo tenor, whose interjections double (or minimally embellish) parts of the top line of the continuous instrumental argument (bb. 46–93). Spasmodic, unobtrusive repetitions of 'y' and an abbreviated variant provide a surface link between sections *A'* and *B*. Most of the remaining *B* material comes from the initial interlocking-third motive in the strings, 'aa' (bb. 46–7), which grows out of the immediately preceding variant of the 'allegiance' motive in bb. 43–5. In bb. 48–51 'aa' is expanded to four bars, then in b. 52 the four-note chromatic descent of b. 50 becomes a separate motive in its own right ('bb'), continually modulating three- and four-bar units embodying reiterations of 'bb' and 'aa' now alternating until the end of b. 68. From b. 69 onwards, 'bb' dominates, its incessant repetitions assuming a triplet rhythm in bb. 78–93. Despite the positive nature of the text in the *B* section, an anxious mood is engendered by the persistent chromaticism and the reappearance in bb. 77–93 of the unsettling trills from the previous two sections.

Part I finishes with a varied reprise of the opening section, which develops the 'allegiance' motive, its abridged derivative ('w') and the yearning chorus 'I believe' ('x'). Section *A''* (bb. 94–119) also introduces in conjunction with the choral statements a solo clarinet motive 'cc', which combines both 'w' and 'x'. The simmering tension of bb. 1–116 is released finally in bb. 117–19 by the appearance of a root-position triad of Ab minor, which is punched out three times. The ensuing ominous two-beat silence is laden with a sense of impending doom.

Bb. 120–248 portray the crucifixion and conclude in the principal structural peak of the whole Mass. To begin with, in section *C* there is a brief elegiac orchestral commentary, hinting at the spiritual aspects of Jesus's forthcoming sacrifice (bb. 120–61). In bb. 120–6 a solo flute expansion ('cc1') of the clarinet motive brought in during the previous section is accompanied by three offstage clarinets (see p. 51), the spatial separation of these four instruments enhancing the other-worldly effect of the music. The three clarinets add their own related rising and falling motive ('dd'), then they enter into a dialogue with the onstage violas and cellos, who vary 'cc'. The clarinet motive gains control in bb. 145–53, the 'accel. e cresc.' marking in bb. 146–7 injecting a little urgency into the proceedings. The forward momentum is increased by the appearance of a 'Più mosso' indication in b. 154 and another 'accel. e cresc.' marking in bb. 156–7 in the offstage clarinets and the onstage violins and violas (bb. 154–61). In bb. 160–1 the cellos and basses, who since b. 145 have been providing a bass line to 'dd', outline a variant of that motive.

The build-up to the focal point of the Mass begins in earnest in b. 162, the start of section *D*. Initially, the positive aspect of the crucifixion – its salvation of mankind – is suggested by a triumphant C major fanfare motive ('ee', a close relative of 'dd') in the horns and trumpets. The fanfare motive is preceded by two statements of only its bass line, which is a rhythmic reinterpretation of the cello and double bass variant of 'dd' in bb. 160–1. During the ensuing sustained *crescendo* (which extends to b. 210) the reiterations of the fanfare are distorted by progressively more dissonant harmonies, the C major triad ultimately being converted into an unstable dominant ninth of F. The fanfare motive also becomes part of an increasingly complex motivic montage. In bb. 179ff. a tortuous, continuous rising line in the strings (formed from trills and 'ff', derived from 'ee') is added to the texture, which is further complicated in bb. 198ff. by irregular interjections of a plunging brass motive ('gg'). The grotesque transformation of the victorious mood of bb. 162–71 into an atmosphere filled with sheer terror is completed in bb. 207–9 by the entry of the side drum, whose roll links section *D* to the 'Raspet' ('Crucifixus').

In section *E* (bb. 210–48 of the published score) 'thunder and flashes of lightning' burst forth from three sets of pedal timpani and the organ (see pp. 52 and 119). A trenchant five-bar timpani motive ('hh', related to 'ff') is four times answered by twisting organ interpolations developing a hectic one-bar chromatic motive ('ii') and its increasingly concise derivatives.[4] The final organ interpolation subsumes the weighty intonation by the chorus (who have been silent for 141 bars) of 'and was crucified also for us, he suffered and was buried'. The full horror of the violent culmination of Jesus's life is then rammed home by a fifth statement of 'hh', which is blasted out on an Ab minor triad by three piccolos, horns, trumpets and trombones, and which is reinforced by a spine-chilling three-timpani roll, as well as by an immense cymbal crash and a *fortissimo* organ chord on its final crotchet beat.

Janáček actually provided programmatic titles for sections *C* and *E* in his initial draft: 'Jesus in the temple among the wise men' and 'the expulsion from the temple of the degenerate traders'. The composer omitted these headings from the final version, presumably considering that the clear changes of mood in the instrumental interlude meant that no verbal explanation was required.

The beginning of the next section (*F*) is superficially the most perplexing moment in the entire work. First, there are eight *fortissimo* bars still in the crucifixion key of Ab minor, played mainly by the strings, who introduce an inert upper- and lower-neighbour-note motive ('jj'). After that, the words 'and on the third day he rose again according to the scriptures' are sung in Ab minor to a variant of 'jj' by the sopranos and altos, whose parts are doubled by three flutes. Vogel's assessment of this apparently puzzling passage, which is that Janáček is aiming 'simply to achieve the necessary contrast', is unhelpful, because there is no contrast of key (1963, 322). Kundera's explanation – that the passage represents a 'secret miracle' – is no more enlightening. In fact, Janáček's conception is infinitely more daring and disturbing than Vogel and Kundera suggest: his almost cinematic setting indicates a sceptical attitude towards the resurrection. Section *E* portrays Jesus's death and the ensuing earthquake, cutting in section *F* to a scene in which the women enter Jesus's tomb and discover that his body has disappeared. Their reaction is not one of euphoria, however, only of bewilderment and incredulity – hence the indecisive circling by the sopranos and altos around the tonic triad of Ab minor. Clearly, Janáček will not be convinced that the resurrection actually happened until he has been able to 'see for himself' (see p. 120). The air of doubt is also underlined by the relatively minor decrease in tension after the focal point of bb. 210–48, and by the build-up in bb. 249–304 to another only slightly less powerful structural peak in bb. 305–16, which function as an after-shock to the 'earthquake' in bb. 244–8.

Motive 'jj' is developed throughout the whole of sections *F* and *F'* (bb. 249–88 and 289–316). The tension is stepped up in bb. 289ff. by a significant increase in tempo (from 'Andante' to 'Allegro') and the appearance of a triplet chorus variant of 'jj' (bb. 290–1 and 301–4). The hysterical setting of 'and his kingdom shall have no end' (bb. 301–4) is eclipsed in bb. 305–13 by five crashing tam-tam strokes, an unresolved V^7 chord of E (embellished by frenzied wind and string trills) in bb. 309–16 further intensifying the atmosphere of anguished uncertainty.

A subsiding timpani roll connects part II and part III (bb. 317–99), which begins *pianissimo* with a substantial reduction of forces and a decrease in tempo to 'Moderato'. At the start of section *A'''* (bb. 317–41) there is a hushed chorus variant of the whole-tone 'I believe' motive over a Cb pedal (bb. 317–20). This is followed in bb. 321–4 by a four-bar choral variant of the sprightly 'allegiance motive' ('v') setting lines 42–3 of the text. Motive 'v' is reduced to two bars, then one, in seven ascending woodwind reiterations (bb. 325–33), these woodwind statements overlapping with a series of rapidly diminishing further choral variants of 'v' that account for lines 44–6 of the text (up to 'is worshipped and glorified'). A last, loosely imitative choral version of 'v' setting 'who spake by the Prophets' (bb. 334–5) is linked to a short, *fortissimo* 'Maestoso' passage employing a final instrumental variant of that motive (bb. 336–40). The closing bars of A''' finally quit the C♭ pedal, moving to V^4_3 of C in b. 340.

The initial, modest accumulation of tension in bb. 317–40 is broken off abruptly in b. 341, where there is a general pause. But the momentum is quickly re-established by an increase in tempo in b. 342 and the appearance of chord I of C with an accompaniment figure formed from a rising arpeggio and repeated quavers. The accompaniment pattern persists throughout the ensuing build-up proper to the final structural peak of the movement (bb. 381–99). Bb. 343–53 of the Coda introduce in the orchestra a jerky, three-bar upper-neighbour-note motive ('kk'), which is repeated three times (once incompletely). The first three statements of 'kk' are embellished by the chorus (bb. 343–5) and the tenor solo (bb. 346–7 and 348–50), who jointly affirm belief in 'one Holy, Catholic and Apostolic Church'. In bb. 354–61 a faster, two-bar ascending-fifth rhythmic derivative ('ll') of the 'one Holy' motive is stated four times by the orchestra, the solo tenor binding the first three of these two-bar units with a florid, expansive six-bar elaboration of 'll', which sets the words 'and I acknowledge one baptism for the remission of sins'. Next, a gradual *accelerando* underlines the combining of a free orchestral rhythmic diminution of 'll' (which is treated imitatively in bb. 366–9) and two choral declarations of 'I look for the resurrection of the dead' that reiterate motive 'kk'.

In b. 370 a drop back to the tempo of b. 342 once again checks the build-up. Motive 'kk' is now presented simultaneously in its original three-bar form (by the orchestra) and in a two-bar variant (by the solo bass to the words 'and the life of the world to come'). A two-bar form of the motive is then played four times by the orchestra, whose statements overlap with two vocal three-bar versions (in the solo bass and the chorus). A powerful increase in orchestral forces underpins bb. 370–80, resulting in a grand, tumultuous 'Amen' passage, in which two four-bar blocks, built from 'll' and its one-bar imitative variant respectively, appear twice in alternation. The movement is rounded off by three E♭ major chords, which are connected by two last instrumental reiterations of the free diminution of 'll'.

Despite the apparently jubilant mood of the closing stages of the 'Věruju', the indecisive swaying throughout the Coda between I of E and I of E♭ adds an undercurrent of uncertainty to the vocalists' declaration of belief in 'the life of the world to come'. This atmosphere of doubt mirrors the much more overt mood of scepticism that dominates the section of the movement dealing with the resurrection, ascension and day of judgement (bb. 249–316).

Svet

Normally, the Sanctus and Benedictus parts of the Mass text (lines 54–6 and 57–8) form the basis of two interlinked movements, the words 'Hosanna in the highest' acting as a refrain and receiving similar (or identical) musical treatment both times that they are sung. The traditional structural pattern can be summarised as *ABCB'*. Janáček, on the other hand, conflates his 'Svet' and 'Blagoslovl'en' and omits the first 'Osana', using what is customarily the second line of the *A* portion of text ('heaven and earth are full of thy glory') for an entire section of music. Consequently, the composer's 'Svet' has an alternative *ABCB'* arrangement, setting lines 54, 55, 57 and 58 of the text. Musically, the *B* and *B'* sections have two main features in common: their frequent repetitions of a brass motive (bb. 39–44 etc.) not employed in the other two sections; and initial tempo markings ('Con moto' and 'Allegro') that are considerably faster than those of *A* and *C* ('Moderato' and 'Meno mosso'). An additional noteworthy feature of this movement's external musical organisation is an explicit link between sections *C* and *B'*: the 'Blagoslovl'en' motive introduced in bb. 105–8 of the former section reappears twice with its original text in the course of the latter (bb. 183–6 and 191–6). On a higher level, the 'Svet' divides into two connected parts (bb. 1–103 and 104–206), each with its own structural peak (bb. 37–90 and 179–97).

At the start of the 'Svet' Janáček once again avoids the obvious. The opening orchestral introduction (bb. 1–17) is not bright and joyful, but ethereal and serene. It begins with an undulating two-bar quaver motive ('mm'), which is scored for violins, harp and celeste, and which is accompanied by gently pulsating repeated crotchets in the cellos and basses. This motive is reiterated three times with minor alterations, each of the last two of these statements also employing slightly different orchestration. In the second half of b. 8 the motive is compressed to only four quavers ('mm1'), and in bb. 10–17 'mm1' assumes a subsidiary role to a blissful, soaring solo violin line constructed from a related three-bar rising motive ('nn') and three ascending statements of a two-bar variant ('nn1'). Bb. 18–20 introduce in the solo soprano a sighing, trifold acclamation of 'Holy' ('oo'), which grows out of the falling sixth in the solo violin in the preceding bar (b. 17). The 'Holy' motive is repeated in bb. 21–5 first by the solo tenor, then by the solo bass. All three vocal utterances in bb. 18–25 are haloed (mainly an octave higher) by the solo violin and are supported by string and woodwind statements of 'mm1'.

In bb. 24–5 the solo bass's intended trifold acclamation of 'Holy' is abridged by one bar and is followed by the beginning of a new subsection of *A* (bb. 26–37). Three motivic levels are brought into play here. These are articulated by the orchestra, chorus and vocal soloists. They are connected by an unbroken line in the solo violin, whose part is a patchwork of components from all three levels. In bb. 26–7 the solo bass sings the second half of the opening line of text ('Lord God of Hosts') to a rising and falling minor-third idea ('pp'). The chorus superimposes a three-bar expansion ('pp1'), which prefaces the original two-bar unit with the falling sixth cell of the 'Holy' motive. At the same time, the orchestra brings in a fresh, more agitated version of the tranquil opening motive of the movement ('mm2'). In bb. 29–32 'pp' is twice repeated (once by the solo soprano and once by the bass) in conjunction with an instrumental restatement of 'mm2' (b. 29–31) and a further variant ('mm3' in bb. 31–2). These two units support a three-bar reprise of 'pp1' in the chorus (bb. 30–2). Section *A* concludes with two instrumental repetitions of 'mm3', together with overlapping vocal statements of 'pp1' (in the solo bass and chorus in bb. 33–5 and 35–7), the second of which overflows into section *B* (bb. 37–103).

The preliminary focal point of the movement (bb. 37–90) sets up a conflict between three tonal areas E, E♭ and D♭/C♯. Throughout this passage two alternating motivic blocks – the first allocated to the orchestra and the second to the chorus and brass – are constantly transposed. The orchestral block comprises a one-bar quaver ostinato ('qq') and a festive three-bar brass fanfare ('rr'), both ideas deriving from the movement's opening motive ('mm'). The other block consists of a two-bar chorus setting of 'heaven and earth are full of thy glory' ('ss', reproducing the intervallic structure of the first half of 'qq') and a three-bar brass variant ('ss1'). Five occurrences of the chorus and brass block interact with five of the orchestral one. The statements of the former are all the same length, while those of the latter encompass eight, seven, twelve, six and six bars respectively. Section *B* ends with a more subdued final six-bar orchestral block on I⁶₄ of E (bb. 91–6), followed by a seven-bar transition based entirely on 'qq' (bb. 97–103). This connecting passage thins out the texture and decelerates towards part II of the movement.

Section C (bb. 104–36) is underpinned by a $IV–I_4^6–V^7–I$ progression in Db. Motivically, this 'Blagoslovl'en' section employs incessant reiterations of the ostinato 'qq' and a half-bar variant ('qq1'), and more irregular, varied repetitions of a vocal idea ('tt'), whose outline of two falling sixths recalls the 'Svet' motive ('oo'). At first, 'tt' is tossed to and fro by the soprano, tenor and bass soloists, the last two of whom increase its length to five bars. The fifth statement (bb. 126–31) comprises imitation between the solo tenor and the solo alto (making her belated first appearance in the work) and spans six bars. An accelerating short transitional passage (bb. 131–6) then steers the harmony towards Eb major.

A faster tempo ('Allegro') is brought in by section B', which introduces two versions of a motive circling around the interval of a minor third: the first ('uu') is a seven-bar instrumental idea (bb. 137–43), and the other ('uu1') is a choral setting of 'Hosanna in the highest' using only the first three bars of 'uu'. In bb. 137–64 'uu' appears four times over an Eb pedal, a chorus 'Hosanna' reinforcing both the second and fourth statements. A general *crescendo* in bb. 162–5 leads to a concerted orchestral build-up in bb. 165–82. Here the Eb pedal persists initially as a support to two further, registrally highlighted reiterations of 'uu' (beginning on ab^3 in the first flute). Then the arrival of chord V^7 of C (bb. 179–82) is underlined by pounding timpani statements of 'qq' and its variant 'qq1', the ostinato dominating the texture for the first time in the movement.

The timpani entry in b. 179 marks the beginning of the principal focal point of the 'Svet' (bb. 179–82, i–xiv and 183–97), which prolongs chord V of F major, the movement's tonal goal. The progress towards tonal resolution is reinforced by motivic integration. Two 4/4 variants of the 'Hosanna' motive ('uu'), the festive brass motive ('rr') and the ostinato ('qq') are all combined in bb. i–xiv and 186–90. Furthermore, two returns of the 'Blagoslovl'en' motive ('tt') are added in bb. 183–6 and 191–7. The tension is discharged by the arrival in b. 198 of I of F, which is prolonged in bb. 199–204 and consolidated by a closing $IV(ii)_5^6–I$ cadence in the last two bars. Motivically, bb. 198–206 also combine 'uu', 'rr' and 'qq'. Only at the end of the last bar does the virtually incessant quaver movement of the 'Svet', which is in effect a *motu perpetuo*, finally cease.

Agneče Božij

After the animated brilliance of the 'Svet', the 'Agneče' reverts to the anguished mood propounded by the 'Gospodi' and much of the 'Věruju'. Janáček renders this final choral movement yet more despondent by reorganising its text: he removes the potentially tranquil phrase 'grant us thy peace', and changes the usual *AAB* textual pattern to *ABA* through the alternation of two different (abbreviated) versions of the remaining distinct line of text ('O Lamb of God, that takest away the sins of the world, have mercy upon us'). Musically, sections *A* and *B* encompass a two-stage build-up to a loud, *espressivo* highpoint in bb. 37–8, the descent from which is interrupted in the ruthlessly abridged *A′* section by a choral outburst swelling from *pianissimo* to *fortissimo*.

Section *A* (bb. 1–23) is constructed from two alternating, thrice-stated blocks, the first containing several repetitions of an instrumental ostinato ('vv'), and the second comprising an essentially *a cappella*, homophonic choral entreaty for forgiveness ('ww'). The four-note, 'Adagio' instrumental motive is a contracted form of the ostinato used in bb. 37–206 of the 'Svet' ('qq'). Its harmonisation by oscillating major-minor-seventh[5] and major-seventh chords, as well as the sombre timbre of its accompanimental lines, establish a melancholy atmosphere. The three-bar choral motive ('ww'), which repeats and varies a basic one-bar unit, has a rising overall contour, but actually ends with a despairing fall through a major third followed by a perfect fourth. It adds an element of desperation to the already subdued mood through its more urgent tempo marking, its *crescendo*, and its highly ambiguous tonal structure. The *A* section derives its impetus from a structural *accelerando* (the ostinato block shortens from seven to five to three bars) and an overall increase in volume.

The gloomy mood of the opening section is intensified in the next – *B* (bb. 24–38). The single motive employed here ('xx') is a two-bar syncopated idea derived from the choral entreaty ('ww'). It is stated initially by the first violins and first clarinet in bb. 24–5, and it is reiterated six times in bb. 26–38. Each of the seven statements of 'xx' – all of which are two bars long, apart from the extended third one – is accompanied by a repeated, compressed half-bar variant ('xx1'). Superimposed on the instrumental statements of 'xx' are six largely overlapping solo vocal utterances of an expanded variant ('xx2'). The pervasive chromaticism and syncopation, as well as the progressively more ambiguous series of harmonies, are underlined by an increase in volume, which is facilitated by the removal of mutes

87

in all instruments bar the trombones. A *fortissimo* highpoint is reached in bb. 37–8 on a triad of A major.

An abridged reprise of *A* (bb. 39–53) – which is linked to section *B* by an overlap in the solo soprano's part – dissipates the tension accumulated in bb. 1–38 only very gradually. This section contains two orchestral blocks (of seven and five bars) employing the ostinato 'vv'. These instrumental passages surround a final choral acclamation of the three-bar plea for forgiveness (bb. 46–8). Each of the orchestral blocks is rounded off by a reiterated plagal cadence in the tonic (Ab minor), the second Ab triad incorporating a Picardy third. Mutes are replaced in b. 39, but the dynamic level subsides slowly, the overall *diminuendo* being interrupted by the chorus's swelling final outburst in bb. 46–8. The lack in this section of a dominant preparation of the closing Ab triad means that this chord has still to be confirmed unequivocally as the tonic of the whole Mass. The tonal instability of the concluding bars further emphasises the movement's general mood of despair.

Organ Solo and Intrada

In the unrelentingly tempestuous Organ Solo that ends the Mass proper, all vestiges of optimism are blown away by an explosion of the crucifixion key: Ab minor. This leaves us in no doubt that Janáček does not believe the solution to the mystery of creation to lie in blind belief in the resurrection and 'the life of the world to come'. To him, the Mass text embodies an essentially human drama of suffering and death. The Organ Solo comes close to matching the power and violence of the 'Raspet' ('Crucifixus') section (bb. 210–48 of the 'Věruju') as it drives furiously towards its final Ab minor chord.

The form of the organ movement is essentially *AA'A''* (bb. 1–39, 40–119, 120–54). Each section develops the opening two-bar motive ('yy'), which appears during the course of the movement in a multitude of forms, different variants frequently being heard in plain or even augmented imitation. The explicit connections of mood and key between this movement and the 'Crucifixus' section of the 'Věruju' are reinforced by the close relationship between their main motives: 'yy' is a chromatic distortion of 'hh'. In the Organ Solo an atmosphere of sheer frenzy is whipped up through an *accelerando* from 'Allegro' through 'Un poco più mosso' and 'Presto' to 'Prestissimo'. The inescapable fact of Jesus's death is forced home tonally by the frequent returns of A♭ minor and the sixfold acclamation of the tonic triad in bb. 146–54.

Vogel describes the ensuing reprise of the Intrada, which would accompany the exit of clergy and congregation from the church in a liturgical performance, as 'a marching entry into life strengthened by a new "certainty" and by the preceding display of the Slav spirit' (1963, 324). However, the superficial optimism of this movement is undermined by the persistent chromaticism (which extends as far as the final cadence) and is overshadowed by the preceding violent, anguished Organ Solo. Thus, although the Intrada does act as a transition back to the real world, it is a march back into a life whose meaning is yet to be discovered.

5

Introduction to the musical organisation

Prefatory remarks

This chapter examines five elements of the Mass: motivic organisation; harmonic language; climactic structure; overall organisation; and word-setting. The Mass's fifty-one main melodic ideas are all quoted in Example 10 on pp. 67–71.

Motivic structure

Janáček's basic constructional unit is the brief thematic fragment, which is usually between four semiquaver beats and three bars long. This unit is essentially a melodic gesture, but it is as a rule supported by one or more accompanying lines. Despite their brevity, Janáček's thematic fragments generally incorporate internal intervallic and/or rhythmic repetition, many comprising two identical or minimally differentiated parts.[1] In addition, most are simple rhythmically; indeed, eleven out of the fifty-one quoted in Example 10 lack rhythmic definition on at least their first appearance and several others have little variety of note values or are dominated by one short repeated rhythmic pattern. Syncopation is scarce ('xx' is unusual in its displacement by a quaver of a reiterated minim–crotchet pattern), and so are anacruses: all but a few melodic fragments begin on or just after the first beat of the bar. As far as shape is concerned, these ideas often revolve around a single note or chord; in fact, many start and finish on the same pitch, embodying an ascending neighbour-note motion (e.g. 'x') or rising and falling skips of a third ('k').

A few of the melodic fragments are monophonic, but most are accompanied by one or more simple figures: held chords, repeated notes, trills, arpeggios, broken chords, doublings of the main line (e.g. at the third, sixth or octave), two alternating harmonies, a sequence of chords over a bass pedal, and so on. There is also some small-scale contrapuntal writing in the

Mass. Several ideas are furnished with countermelodies on at least one occasion, and eleven units are echoed (largely at the octave or unison) after a bar or half-bar on one or more of their appearances. Another polyphonic procedure employed in the work is heterophony. Characteristic uses of this technique can be found in bb. 3–6 of the 'Slava', where a twice-stated instrumental unit ('m') overlaps with a more elaborate variant in the solo soprano, and in bb. 7–9 etc. of the 'Úvod', in which two motives ('d' and 'e') with identical intervallic structures but completely different rhythmic organisations are superimposed.

All but a tiny minority of the fifty-one thematic fragments are accorded a mono-chordal harmonic setting. Thus the source of dynamism in the work is to be discovered not in the fragments themselves, but in the way they are transposed, varied, juxtaposed and superimposed within an ever-changing montage. But, before we investigate the methods by which Janáček builds up sections of music, we need to devise a name for his principal unit of construction. Possible labels are 'phrase', 'theme' and 'motive'. Schoenberg defines these three clearly (1967, 1–22). A 'phrase' is the 'smallest structural unit' of a piece, 'consisting of a number of integrated musical events' and possessing 'a certain completeness'. Two or more phrases make up a 'theme', which is a 'complete musical idea' with a 'definite ending'. A phrase may itself incorporate one or more short 'motives'. A motive is not an autonomous structural entity, but it does delineate 'a memorable shape' implying 'an inherent harmony'. Also, it is repeated and varied from phrase to phrase and is the 'smallest common multiple of a piece'. Obviously, Schoenberg would have considered Janáček's basic units too fragmentary to warrant the label 'phrase' or 'theme'. But his term 'motive' is not entirely suitable either, because Janáček's units often incorporate internal repetition. Fortunately, William Drabkin's broader definition of 'motive' is more appropriate: he states simply that a motive is a 'short utterance that retains its identity as a musical idea' (1987, 122). We can therefore call Janáček's fragments 'motives' according to this less specific definition. As for the smaller intervallic patterns within the motives, we can term these 'cells', Drabkin stating that a 'cell' is a unit that is 'still smaller' than a motive.

Every movement of the Mass (with the exception of the Intrada) divides into three or more sections. Each new section has a substantially different motivic arrangement from the preceding one and usually begins with a striking change of tempo and/or time-signature. All sections use from one to five motives, most employing two or three. Within a section each motive is repeated and subjected to several transformations, the disposition of, as well as the interaction between, the various forms of all the motives determining the section's overall shape. Let us first consider how an individual motive might be utilised in a section. To begin with, it may be repeated at the same pitch in part or in its entirety. But, since Janáček's motives largely have mono-chordal settings, this procedure can mainly only be used to prolong a single harmony. For meaningful harmonic progressions to be effected, each motive in a section must undergo several transpositions. Similarly, because sections of music are a patchwork of short repeated fragments, constant modification of the salient intervals of each motive in subsequent restatements is necessary to create a sense of melodic continuity on a large scale. For instance, in bb. 3–19 of the 'Slava', the initial bars of the first statement of 'k' (b. 3) and of each of the succeeding three transpositions of this motive (bb. 9, 16 and 18) are connected by the gradual expansion of the opening interval from a major third to a minor sixth and at the same time by the phased contraction of the final interval from a major sixth to a minor second. Temporary reverses within these processes add further interest. For example, before the initial interval of 'k' grows from a major third to a fifth, there is a deceptive narrowing of this interval to a minor third (b. 9).

Over the course of a complete section a motive generally spawns one or more full 'variants'. Janáček's most common methods of varying a motive include addition and omission of notes, modification of the duration of some pitches, conversion of duplet patterns to triplet ones and vice versa, a change of time-signature, insertion or removal of internal rests, and alteration of several intervals to suggest a completely different harmonic outline. Variants, like the original motives, are also often stated several times, their repetitions frequently being linked by gradual expansions and/or contractions of important intervals. Moreover, all the variants of a motive in a section are usually embraced by further large-scale processes. For example, in bb. 1–32 of the Intrada motive 'b' is shortened progressively, its variants reducing from six through four and three to two minims.

Though a section may employ up to five motives, no more than three are in operation at a time. Hence a section's texture consists of one to three 'levels', or 'strata'. Each level comprises a series of motives of continually fluctuating length, along with any accompanimental lines (homophonic or contrapuntal). Levels may be used continuously or intermittently, and they can clash or overlap. In addition, two or three levels sounding simultaneously may be equal in prominence or arranged hierarchically. Where strata have relative degrees of importance, we can call them 'primary', 'secondary' and 'tertiary'. A motive may be transferred from a lower level to a higher one and vice versa – a motive and one of its variants may even be part of different levels on occasions. Bb. 1–38 of the 'Slava' illustrate perfectly how structural levels and motives function independently. This section uses three motives ('k', 'l' and 'm'), but only two strata (primary and secondary). Bb. 1–23 introduce 'k' on the primary level, heterophonic variants and two accompanimental patterns supporting several statements of this motive. In b. 23 'l' and an abbreviated variant enter in imitation on the secondary level, brushing 'k' aside in the very next bar. The promotion of 'l' to the primary level lasts only four bars, after which it retires to the secondary one, having been displaced by 'm' (a derivative of 'k').

Janáček's highly individual and flexible method of creating continuous passages of music through a fluctuating motivic montage has the potential for producing a very wide variety of sectional arrangements. Nevertheless, some basic ground-plans do occur several times. A particularly common scheme involves the alternation of two motivic blocks. In bb. 37–96 of the 'Svet', for example, two contrasting blocks are juxtaposed repeatedly: the first (orchestral) block is made up of two strata (primary and secondary) occupied by 'rr' and 'qq' respectively; the second comprises 'ss' in the chorus and a brass and percussion variant. There are five statements altogether of the 'ss' block, which is modified by transposition alone. This section is shaped by variations in the length of the other motivic block, whose six appearances encompass eight, seven, twelve, six, six and six bars.

Another element imparting coherence to a section is the interrelationship of many or all of its motives. Bb. 1–17 of the 'Úvod' bring in three motives ('d', 'e' and 'f'), which are all related: 'e' is a reinterpretation of the intervallic content of 'd'; and 'f' begins with the pattern of a rising followed by a falling minor third that is outlined by the fourth, fifth and sixth notes of 'd'. The existence of close motivic relationships in all sections means that my criteria for distinguishing between a 'variant' and a new 'motive' require explanation. If two units have only certain intervallic cells and/or rhythmic patterns in common, and if they otherwise differ sharply in overall contour, orchestration, the style of their accompaniments and so on, they are deemed to be separate motives. A 'variant' must have features in common with its parent unit in two or more musical dimensions, and it should preserve the original order of intervallic and rhythmic events (even if some components are omitted). Admittedly, there are some awkward cases, notably motives 'd' and 'e'. Many writers on the Mass view 'e' as a variant of 'd' (see, for example, Vogel 1963, 319). I prefer to consider them as distinct, related motives because, though they have the same essential intervallic structure, they are completely unalike in all other respects (rhythm, metre, orchestration etc.).

On a larger scale, multi-sectional movements in the Mass are governed superficially by substantial returns of material, which create the elementary repetitive sectional patterns encountered throughout Janáček's oeuvre: the 'Gospodi' and 'Agneče' are *ABA'*; the 'Svet' is *ABCB'*; the 'Úvod', 'Slava' and 'Věruju' are loose rondos; and the Organ Solo is essentially *AA'A''*. Some of these schemes are prescribed by the text (e.g. that of the 'Gospodi'), but, interestingly, the composer reorganised the texts of the 'Věruju' and 'Agneče' to produce his favourite ternary and rondo schemes; the surface rondo structure of the 'Slava' is even added in structural counterpoint to the fundamental binary arrangement suggested by the text. Groups of successive sections, like individual ones, are unified by long-term motivic procedures. In particular, returns of material in a movement are usually connected by an ongoing process: e.g. *A'* and *A''* in the 'Slava' integrate increasingly thoroughly all the main motivic material introduced up to the point at which they begin. Indeed, most movements exhibit a trend towards motivic synthesis within and between sections. In the 'Gospodi', not only are motives 'g' and 'h' combined as early as b. 11 in section *A* (bb. 1–36), but the final section – *A'* (bb. 76–90) – integrates material from both *A* and *B*. Such large-scale procedures are usually reinforced by motivic overlaps. In the 'Gospodi', the first two sections are linked by the premature appearance in b. 29 of motive 'i' (which is used throughout section *B*); and the last two are connected by a half-bar overlap between 'i' in bb. 75–6 and the return of 'g' at the beginning of b. 76.

A further factor that underlines the general trend of progressive motivic integration over the course of a movement is the interrelationship of at least the principal ideas from section to section. For example, in the first two sections of the 'Slava' (bb. 1–38 and 39–68), rising fourths and fifths abound. The ascending fourth cell heard in b. 1 reappears prominently in the accompaniment to motive 'm' (b. 28) and then grows to a fifth within 'l' (b. 39), thereafter occurring in both forms in further variants of 'm' (e.g. in bb. 57 and 60). Furthermore, the expanded version of this cell is employed in the third section of the movement (bb. 69–86): it occurs at the beginning of 'n' and of that motive's variants, even concluding the whole section.

The three largest movements (the 'Slava', 'Věruju' and 'Svet') have an extra unit of formal division that is larger than a section. In these movements, groups of interlinked sections are separated by general pauses or other very strongly marked structural breaks. Such groups of sections may be termed 'parts', the 'Slava' and 'Svet' comprising two parts and the 'Věruju' three. This principle can be exemplified briefly with reference to the 'Slava'. The first three sections are connected by a motivic overlap in bb. 38–9 and a transitional passage at the end of the second section (bb. 66–8), whereas after b. 86 there is an emphatic motivic, rhythmic, textural and dynamic break accompanied by a sudden drop in tension and momentum. Thus b. 87 marks the beginning of the second part, which also incorporates three sections (bb. 87–138, 139–80 and 181–228) linked by a three-bar transition (bb. 136–8) and a motivic overlap (bb. 180–1). Naturally, adjacent parts of movements are also by and large interconnected motivically: the rising fifth cell of b. 86 of the 'Slava' is repeated immediately in b. 87 at the start of motive 'o', and it goes on to dominate 'r'.

If we discount the reappearance of the Intrada at the end of the work, there are no significant reprises of material from movement to movement. There are only some fleeting, subsidiary recalls of individual motives. For instance, motive 'i' (used in the 'Gospodi') is recalled in the soprano part in bb. 9–10 of the 'Slava', and the important and distinctive falling sixth motive ('oo') of bb. 18–20 etc. of the 'Svet' is prefigured in b. 13 of the 'Slava' and recalled in bb. 29–30 of the 'Agneče'. It is difficult to ascertain whether these minor recurrences of material were deliberate, but they are so limited in scope that they scarcely constitute a major organisational factor.

A more thorny question is that of whether motivic unity exists in the Mass as a whole. The multiplicity of intervallic connections within movements has encouraged most commentators to concentrate almost exclusively on searching for a cell or small group of cells that is/are common to all the work's main motives. Both Hans Hollander and Karl Wörner (in a piece largely about *Kát'a Kabanová*) claim to have found a single generative cell, which consists of a descending major second followed by a falling perfect fourth (Hollander 1963, 129; and Wörner 1969, 153). They label this pattern 'basic formula' (*Grundformel*) and 'module' (*Modell*) respectively. Unfortunately, Hollander does not expound his theory in detail and Wörner has to permit an impossibly wide range of 'modular variants' (*Modellvarianten*): the basic cell may be stated in inversion, retrograde or retrograde inversion; and either interval may be expanded or contracted. Thus all Wörner is in fact asserting is that in the Mass (as well as in *Kát'a*) all the motives incorporate two consecutive descending or ascending intervals. Banal though this observation is, many important motives in the Mass contradict it: 'j', 'q', 'r', 'w', 'x' etc. do not include any variant of Wörner's module. Clearly, anybody wishing to demonstrate that the *Glagolitic Mass* is unified motivically must adopt a different approach.

Jaroslav Vogel's evaluation of the issue is a little more penetrating (1963, 319). He pinpoints three 'motivic elements' (*motivické prvky*), each comprising three notes: (a) the descending second and fourth cell identified by Hollander and Wörner; (b) a rising and falling third pattern; and (c) an upper-neighbour-note figure. Realistically, he also allows a much narrower range of variation: (a) must retain a downward contour, even though either interval can be expanded or compressed; and (b) and (c) can each outline either the major or the minor form of its interval (third and second respectively). Vogel's two additional cells are employed more often and much more prominently than the Hollander/Wörner cell: one or the other actually forms part of the opening orchestral motive and the initial vocal utterance of nearly every movement. Moverover, unlike (a), whose infrequent appearances are highly localised, (b) and (c) often dictate the contour of a whole motive. Example 11 shows motive 'k' (from bb. 3–4 of the 'Slava'), which delineates cell (a) at the end of its first bar, but which as a whole outlines (c) – the neighbour-note figure.

Despite Vogel's more flexible approach, his brief examination of motivic coherence in the Mass is still far from satisfactory. First, none of his 'motivic elements' can be found in a number of the work's most important melodic fragments (notably 'r'). Second, some other cells are actually much more significant than his cell (a): for example, the rising fifth pattern used at many points in the 'Slava'. And third, a supposed variant of (a) – falling third followed by descending fourth – actually appears frequently enough to be classified as a cell in its own right.

Another possible line of investigation is to search for a *Grundgestalt*

Ex. 11

Ex. 12

('basic shape'). This term (devised by Schoenberg) denotes the principal idea of a piece, which contains all its essential material and is normally two to three bars long. Of course, we face the initial difficulty of determining which of Janáček's motives is the Mass's *Grundgestalt*: do we take as our model the initial idea of the 'Úvod' (the first movement in the published score) or that of the Intrada (the first movement of Janáček's own preferred arrangement)? The former would appear to have more potential as a 'basic shape', so let us examine its structure. We can subdivide this motive into at least four salient components, as is demonstrated by Example 12. Cells (a) and (b), the rising fifth and an expansion of the falling third plus fourth pattern are all there, but what of cell (c) and the falling fourth and rising third pattern that plays such a major role (in its original form and in retrograde inversion) in motives 'q', 'v', 'w' and several others? We could get round the problem of accounting for all the Mass's motivic material by proposing that the opening motives of the Intrada and 'Úvod' are each part of a corporate *Grundgestalt*, but surely this is more than a little far-fetched. And even if we did countenance such a dubious line of argument, further researches would reveal that the most commonly encountered cells in the work are simply elements of Janáček's style and are by no means exclusive to the *Glagolitic Mass*. For example, Dietmar Ströbel shows that the upper-neighbour-note figure, (c), underlies many major motives in Janáček's works written in the period c. 1894–1911 (1975, 27–45).

Thus for a convincing, if tantalisingly succinct, assessment of the matter we must turn to Carl Dahlhaus, who writes in relation to Janáček's operas (1985, 97):

> The term 'monothematicism' has urged itself upon some exegetes [e.g. Hollander] when they have been trying to characterize the role of motivic technique in Janáček's musical dramaturgy. It is an overstatement, but a helpful and illuminating one, for there is no escaping the impression that an opera by Janáček rests on a network of motivic relationships which is steadily drawn tighter and tighter.

If we adopt this undogmatic approach towards the *Glagolitic Mass*, we can discover the reason why it appears unified motivically. It is the integration and concentration of each movement's most prominent motives towards its close that create the impression that all the work's motives are related intervallically. Certainly, the 'network of motivic relationships' in the final section of the 'Slava' (bb. 181–228) could hardly be 'drawn tighter'. First, motives 'k' and 'r' (embodying the most important cells of parts I and II of the movement respectively) are stated simultaneously, 'k' already incorporating the quadruplet rhythmic pattern employed in much part II material. Then a variant of 'r' infiltrates the bass line of the accompaniment to 'k' (bb. 185–6). This union creates a new, shorter motive ('u'), which isolates three pitches of 'k', is accompanied by a variant of 'r', and reverses the contour of 't' (the motive that dominates bb. 139–80 of the movement). Having been introduced, motive 'u' is ruthlessly compressed, until in bb. 222–5 it has been abbreviated to a three-crotchet timpani figure comprising two falling fourths. Janáček's parting shot is to reduce this figure to a single note (E) in his final threefold acclamation of the tonic triad.

Harmonic language

In harmonic terms, the Mass continues the nineteenth- and early twentieth-century trend of expanding the fundamental relations of common-practice tonality. But the work is undeniably less experimental (if no less individual) harmonically than much of the music written around the same time, because it maintains an unfashionably sharp distinction between consonance and dissonance. In contrast to many of his contemporaries, Janáček allows only a narrow range of basic consonances: the major and minor triads – each of which may be embellished by an added sixth and/or ninth – and the dominant seventh in root position, which of course had been treated widely by composers as a consonance from the second half of the nineteenth century onwards. (Janáček's striking substitution of a sharpened fourth for the fifth of an E major triad at the end of the 'Gospodi' is unique within the Mass.) Even 6-4 chords, which sometimes appear in parallel chains, resolve eventually on to root-position triads. All this does not mean that Janáček was ultra-conservative in his tolerance of dissonance (in fact his dissonance threshold increased progressively throughout his career), but simply that the wide variety of more adventurous vertical complexes in the *Glagolitic Mass* ultimately enhance, rather than disrupt, its underlying tonal framework.

The dissonant combinations occurring most frequently in the work are, in addition to 6-4 chords, as follows (most of these harmonies are used in different inversions): diminished, half-diminished, major, minor, and major-minor sevenths, as well as seventh chords comprising the intervals (in relation to the bass) of a major third, an augmented fifth and a major seventh; dominant ninths, elevenths and thirteenths; major and minor ninths; augmented triads and other chromatically altered sixth chords (e.g. the 'German sixth'); whole-tone and nearly-whole-tone configurations; and a range of transient vertical dissonances produced by multiple appoggiaturas or passing notes sounding simultaneously. Rarer and yet harsher dissonances, such as bitriadic chords, are usually the result of staggered part movement or the temporary clashing of motivic strata and are sometimes accorded elaborate resolution (see, for example, bb. 64–75 of the 'Úvod').

As a rule, a short sequence of functionally related chords provides the framework of a section (or group of sections). During the course of a complete movement a related series of these large-scale progressions gradually surrounds then consolidates a single tonal goal, which is never defined unequivocally at the outset, and which is often affirmed only at a very late stage. The basic tonal structure of a movement is expanded either by non-functional chains of parallel chords (usually dissonances) or by irregular and ambiguous successions of consonant and dissonant combinations. The final element of the underlying tonal process governing a movement is normally a prolonged (and frequently elaborated) authentic cadence in the tonic (generally I_4^6–V^7–I), which constitutes the most important and emphatic harmonic event in the movement. Major authentic cadences can be found near the close of the Intrada (bb. 36–43), 'Úvod' (bb. 64–75), 'Gospodi' (bb. 76–87), 'Slava' ('bb. 190–7), 'Svet' (bb. 179–82, i–xiv and 183–98) and Organ Solo (bb. 111–26), in these keys respectively: Ab major, E major, E major, E major, F major and Ab minor. (There are specific reasons for the absence of authentic cadences from the final stages of the 'Věruju' and 'Agnece', which are revealed in the examination of the whole work's tonal scheme on pp. 108–11.) Once the tonic of a movement has been asserted unambiguously, Janáček is able to explore subsidiary (mainly plagal) cadential progressions: e.g. IV^6–I (bb. 44–7 of the Intrada), $IV(ii)_5^6$–I (bb. 205–6 of the 'Svet') and bVI^6–I (bb. 48–9 of the Intrada).

Now that the principles of Janáček's harmonic technique in the Mass have been outlined, we can analyse an individual movement in more detail. Example 13 summarises the harmonic plan of the 'Gospodi'. All chords are

Ex. 13

shown on one stave for ease of reference and bar numbers are included. Chords employing unfilled notes are deemed to be the harmonic pillars of the movement; those using filled notes are considered subsidiary. Janáček's wayward use of accidentals is largely retained, although some particularly confusing configurations (e.g. the first chord of b. 28) are simplified.

The tonic of the 'Gospodi' is E major. There are two large-scale progressions – in bb. 1–28(first beat) and 28(second beat)–90 – which both proceed from a half-diminished seventh on B♭ (in root position, then in third inversion) to a root-position E major triad. In the first progression we are invited to hear the E triad as VI of G♯ minor (= A♭ minor). However, as the second one unfolds, the G♯ minor tonal region proves to have been an initial tonicisation of the third of the E major triad, which is consolidated firmly by an embellished I⁶₄–V–I cadence in E in bb. 76–87. This basic plan of concealing the harmonic goal of a movement by first establishing a triad on another degree of the tonic scale is used throughout the Mass. Janáček's scheme derives from a standard nineteenth-century formula where the initial affirmation of the tonic is omitted and a piece therefore appears to start in the 'wrong' key. We can in turn trace that formula back to at least Chopin's Prelude in A minor, Op. 28 no. 2, which begins on V of A minor and embarks on a I⁶₄–V–I cadence in the tonic as late as bar 15 of 23.

Janáček's preliminary large-scale progression in the 'Gospodi' (bb. 1–28) is ii^7–i–VI in Ab/G♯ minor (the notation hovers between these two enharmonic equivalents). The ii^7 chord is preceded briefly by V^0_9 of Ab/G♯ minor (i.e. a diminished seventh on G).[2] The second chord of this progression is followed in the latter part of b. 16 by ii(IV)^6_5 of E, which becomes ii(IV)^2 of the same key in bb. 18–20. But the E major tendencies are negated immediately by a sudden harmonic dislocation in b. 21: chord ii of Ab minor returns and is succeeded rapidly by an added-ninth chord of Ab major in second inversion. At the end of the first main harmonic progression of the movement E major is approached twice through I^6_4 of Ab – i.e. via a triad built on its third degree (bb. 26–8). Hence the initial large-scale harmonic motion in the 'Gospodi' (from Ab/G♯ to E) is inconclusive.

The second (more expansive) underlying progression of the movement begins on the second beat of b. 28. While the violas, cellos and basses are holding the final E major chord of the previous harmonic succession for the first minim bear of b. 28, the woodwind set about re-establishing the opening half-diminished-seventh chord of the movement. The latter achieve their goal with the minimum of fuss, treating E major in first inversion as VI^6 of Ab minor and moving swiftly through V^4_3 and III of that key to ii^7 – the half-diminished seventh on Bb. They then reiterate this pattern in b. 29, holding the final ii^7 chord until the end of b. 36. The whole process is accompanied by an Ab pedal in the horns and violas. Thus in bb. 28–36 the woodwind, horns and violas together sustain the half-diminished seventh in third inversion. In this new form (ii^2 as opposed to ii^7) the half-diminished seventh casts its shadow as far as the first half of b. 56. Two appearances of it (bb. 28–36 and 53–6) frame, and initially clash with, a chain of major-, minor- and dominant-seventh harmonies. The roots of the intervening seventh chords actually delineate the top three of the four notes that make up the half-diminished seventh on Bb (Bb–Db–Fb–Ab). To summarise, the opening chord of the second large-scale progression in the 'Gospodi' is prolonged in vertical and linear dimensions for a total of twenty-eight bars.

In bb. 56–8 there is a decisive change of tonal direction. The arrival of I^6_4 of E major with an added C♯ initiates an authentic cadence in E, whose completion is nevertheless stretched out over more than twenty bars. To begin with, the I^6_4 chord of E (plus an added C♯) is followed in b. 59 by ii(IV)^6_5 and then by a third-inversion dominant seventh (with an added G♯) of that key. These events do indeed suggest that an affirmation of the root-position triad of E major is imminent. However, despite the D♯–E motion in bb. 64–5 in the solo soprano, the chorus and orchestra stubbornly refuse to abandon their dominant harmony, only giving way when the solo soprano has moved on to A, a pitch now supported by an ambiguous whole-tone subset comprising four notes (G–B–F–A) of a dominant ninth of C major (bb. 67–70). The apex of this harmonic excursion is a *fortissimo*, complete whole-tone hexachord on G♭ (bb. 72–5).

After the whole-tone outburst, harmonic equilibrium is restored by the return of I_4^6 of E with an added C♯ (a configuration first introduced in bb. 56–9). This is no arbitrary event; it is inevitable, not only because of the large-scale progressions that have hitherto outlined E major as the movement's tonal goal, but also owing to linear processes at work since b. 1. The movement's most important long-range linear successions are two overlapping rising chains in the bass, one of thirds and the other of fourths. The first of these delineates a diminished triad on G followed by the tonic triad of E: G (bb. 1–3) is succeeded by B♭ (bb. 4ff.), C♯/D♭ (bb. 16–17 and 37ff.), E (b. 52), A♭ (b. 53) and B (bb. 56–7 and 76–8), hence suggesting completion by a concluding ascent of a fourth to the root of the E major triad. The second chain (of fourths) begins on A♭ in b. 16 and moves to C♯/D♭ in bb. 37ff. It then omits a step (G♭) by proceeding directly to B (bb. 56–9) and progressing via E (bb. 59–61) to A (bb. 62–70). Having overshot its mark, it returns to the missing degree (G♭) and then comes to rest on B as part of chord I_4^6 of E major (bb. 76–8), once again indicating completion by a resolution on to E. Thus the I_4^6 chord of E in bb. 76–8 unites the various harmonic and linear strands of the movement and resolves all of them when it moves via V on to I of E in b. 87.

The closing embellished I_4^6–V–I cadence of the 'Gospodi' (bb. 76–90) is modified in some significant respects. To start with, the dominant chord (bb. 83–4) has two added notes (sixth and ninth) and also leaves out the third (the significance of that omission is considered on p. 109). In addition, chords I_4^6 and V are divided by four bars (79–82) of C major, and chords V and I are separated by two bars (85–6) of the tonic minor. The former tonal digression ties up a loose end; just as the whole-tone configuration in bb. 72–5 is reconciled with the tonic through an F♯–B–E motion in the bass, so the whole-tone subset in bb. 67–70 (suggesting V^9 of C) is resolved on to E via C major and V of E (with which C major has a Neapolitan relationship). A final noteworthy alteration of the concluding cadential formula occurs in the very last bar (90): A♯ replaces B in what has begun in b. 87 as a plain E major chord. This change produces another whole-tone subset (E—G♯–A♯), which colours rather than negates the movement's resolution on to I of E, and which serves three main functions: it refers back to the peak of tonal tension in bb. 72–5; it acknowledges retrospectively the important role in the movement of the half-diminished seventh first stated in b. 4, since this whole-tone subset actually comprises the enharmonic equivalents of three of the four notes (F♭, A♭ and B♭) that make up the half-diminished seventh; and it combines the roots of the only three unadorned root-position triads employed in the movement – E (bb. 26–8 and 87), G♯ (bb. 16–17) and B♭/A♯ (bb. 21–2).

Like the long-term motivic procedures in the 'Gospodi', the large-scale harmonic progressions in this movement unfold across, and overlap with, sectional divisions. The second progression both starts before the beginning of section B and overrides the superficial line of demarcation between sections B and A'. Indeed, the motivic and harmonic processes of the 'Gospodi' operate conjunctly. Not only are the motivic overlaps in bb. 29–36 and 75–6 reinforced by the movement's harmonic scheme, but the combining of motives 'g' and 'h' in bb. 11 and 14 is marked by the clarification of the function of the half-diminished seventh chord on B♭ as a substitute dominant of A♭ minor. The integration of material from sections A and B in the final section (A') is also highlighted by the simultaneous resolution of the movement's various harmonic and linear processes. Elsewhere in the Mass, motivic and harmonic procedures sometimes work in structural counterpoint to one another. For example, the consolidation of the tonic of the 'Slava' (also E major) begins in bb. 190–7, significantly later than the start in b. 181 of the final process of motivic synthesis.

A distinctive feature of the 'Gospodi', and of the Mass in general, is the tension arising between the modal tendencies of some melodic lines and the tonal implications of their surrounding harmonic framework. This type of conflict can be discovered, for instance, in bb. 23–5 of the 'Gospodi'. Here an added-ninth chord of A♭ major in second inversion is decorated by a pentatonic melodic line centred around B♭ – the non-harmonic note of the accompanying vertical sonority. Bb. 3–6 of the 'Slava' are slightly more complex in this respect. The basis of this passage is I$^6_4$ of E♭, which alternates with a minor seventh of B♭, and which eventually proves to be the first component of a large-scale V$^6_4$–i–VI progression in A♭ minor. It is embellished by a pentatonic motive in the clarinet ('k') and a pentatonic heterophonic variant in the solo soprano, which revolve around E♭ and B♭ respectively. Moreover, all the notes employed in bb. 1–6 of the movement make up the Mixolydian mode on Eb. The modal colouring of this passage plays a significant role in imparting naive rapture to the solo soprano's acclamation 'Glory to God in the highest'.

Of course, Janáček's use of modal elements in the Mass extends beyond the pentatonic scale and the so-called 'Church modes'; it even occasionally has a disruptive effect. Particularly striking is the part played by modal inflections in the subversion and eventual dismissal of the dominant of F major in bb. 162–209 of the 'Věruju'. In purely vertical terms this passage progresses from a plain C major triad to a dominant ninth on C via an irregular and increasingly dissonant series of embellished major, minor, whole-tone and diminished-seventh harmonies. But, melodically, the various harmonic areas between the two main pillars of the passage (V and V^9 of F) are connected by a virtually unbroken, modally inflected line in the strings, who play mainly in unison. After ten bars of unpolluted C major, the strings engineer moves to E minor (bb. 173–5) and Gb major (bb. 176–8), thereby introducing a linear whole-tone element. The strings then change tack, first delineating a step-by-step ascent from the dominant to the tonic of F♯ major (C♯–D♯–E♯–F♯), before returning circuitously to C (b. 191). Next they ascend through an entire 'artificial' heptatonic scale (i.e. a seven-note scale with no label in general usage): C–D–E–F♯–G–Ab–Bb. This comprises the first four degrees of the Lydian mode and the last three of the Aeolian. Its prolonged final degree coincides in b. 208 with a brass and woodwind statement of the initial fanfare motive ('ee') outlining V^9 of F. Significantly, the dominant-ninth chord contains five notes (C–E–G–Bb–D) of the artificial scale, the other two of which (F♯ and Ab) appear as accented appoggiaturas. This ambiguous configuration reduces the expectation of an authentic cadence in F major and facilitates a deceptive continuation on to a Db major triad, which deflects the course of the movement towards Ab minor (bb. 210–48 of the published score – but see p. 52 and Example 7). Thus, although modal inflections in the Mass are localised and essentially decorate the underlying tonal structure, they enrich substantially and intensify the work's already highly individual musical language.

Climactic structure

The long-term motivic and harmonic procedures governing individual movements are emphasised powerfully and sometimes linked by underlying climactic processes. Every movement centres around one, two or

three focal points into which its 'various strands coalesce and thereby ma.
a strong emotional impact' (Agawu 1984, 159; he is commenting on
nineteenth- and early twentieth-century music in general). All these structural peaks are preceded by powerful build-ups of tension and most are
followed by sudden or gradual releases of this accumulated pressure. The
work's basic climactic unit – comprising ascent, highpoint and descent –
can be depicted by the shape shown in Figure 1, which is labelled a
'dynamic curve' by Leonard Ratner (1957, 249). In common with
Janáček's other large-scale procedures, his dynamic curves frequently
encompass two or more sections. Indeed, because the ebb and flow of
tension within a movement is always associated with fluctuations in the
readily comprehensible musical dimensions of tempo, register and the
volume of sound, the dynamic curves are, as far as the listener is concerned, the principal determinant of continuity on the highest structural
level.

The ascending part of a curve may exceed ninety bars in length and is
articulated in several dimensions simultaneously. This can be illustrated
with reference to bb. 120–209 of the 'Věruju', the instrumental build-up to
that movement's second high region (the focal point of the entire Mass).
Tension is accumulated here in six principal dimensions. First, and most
obviously, there is a sustained *crescendo* from *piano* (b. 120) through a
general level of *forte* (bb. 162ff.) to *fortissimo* plus (at least in the brass and
strings) after b. 196 (Janáček's dynamic markings are somewhat haphazard
here). This growth in volume is underlined by a gradated augmentation of
orchestral forces and progressively faster tempo markings. It is also

...phasised by staged increases in textural and motivic complexity, and in harmonic and modal ambiguity. Finally, there are two major registral ascents: the uppermost line in the overall texture rises from the c^1 octave in b. 120 to the c^4 octave when piccolos 1 and 2 enter in bb. 204–6 and 208; and the strings delineate a bipartite ascent, from db^2 to $f\sharp^2$ in bb. 179–86, then from c^2 to bb^2 in bb. 191–209. Elsewhere in the work, temporary checks are sometimes employed in build-ups to enhance their effect. For example, the build-up in bb. 317–80 of the 'Věruju' to that movement's final structural peak is interrupted fleetingly, first by a one-bar general pause (b. 341) and later by a drop in volume to *mezzo-forte* (b. 370). On each occasion, the forward momentum is rapidly re-established and then stepped up.

Often the culmination of the ascending portion of a curve lasts for only a few bars, briefly sustaining dynamic and registral peaks over a single unresolved harmony, for instance. A passage of music of this type can be called a 'highpoint'. Bb. 72–5 of the 'Gospodi' are a clear example. These *fortissimo* bars are founded on a highly unstable whole-tone hexachord on Bb, which constitutes the peak of tonal tension in the movement. Elsewhere in the work, focal points are quite frequently much lengthier (some even lasting more than thirty bars); such passages can be allotted the label 'high region'. Examples are bb. 381–99 of the 'Věruju' and bb. 179–97 of the 'Svet'. Both these peaks are prolonged principally in the harmonic dimension, the first by oscillation between chords built on roots a semitone apart, and the second by a protracted resolution on to I of F major.

The descent from a highpoint or high region may also be either abrupt or drawn out. In the 'Úvod' a highpoint is reached in bb. 73–4 on a dominant thirteenth of E, and this is followed by a rapid, forceful discharge of tension in the closing three-bar consolidation of E major (bb. 75–7). In contrast, the descent from the highpoint of the 'Gospodi' (bb. 72–5) is much more gradual. Although the tonal goal of the movement is obvious by b. 76, its arrival is delayed until b. 87. The most lengthy descent from a high region in the Mass occurs in bb. 249–316 of the 'Věruju'. The huge build-up 12–209 of that movement is succeeded by the most powerful ... the work (equivalent to bb. 210–48 of the published score). The ... a build ... b. 249 by a modest decrease in tension and then ... us bb. 210 ..., slightly less powerful peak in bb. 305–16. ... b. 210 ... beginning of after-shock to the shattering high region ... structural peak dissipating finally only at

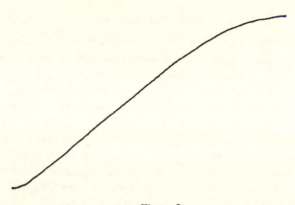

Figure 2

Sometimes, there is no descent from a focal point, a pattern that can be represented by the truncated dynamic curve shown in Figure 2. This type of climactic arrangement occurs when a movement, or a part of a movement, ends with a sustained high region. Abbreviated curves can be found, for instance, in bb. 317–99 of the 'Věruju' and bb. 1–86 of the 'Slava'.

Movements with only one focal point may embody either of the first two basic types of curve: (1), the model with a brief descent (Intrada, Organ Solo and 'Úvod'); and (2), the model with a protracted descent ('Gospodi' and 'Agneče'). The truncated type of curve – model (3) – is not found here. Movements incorporating two ('Slava' and 'Svet') or three ('Věruju') curves may use any of the three models, their high regions and highpoints varying in impact. For example, the 'Svet' contains two curves based on model (1): the first comprises a build-up (bb. 1–36), a prolonged high region (bb. 37–90) and a shortish descent (bb. 91–103); and the other consists of a longer and more powerful build-up (bb. 104–78), a more emphatic high region (bb. 179–97) and a brief discharge of tension (bb. 198–206). Thus the overall shape of the movement (with the main peak near the end) mirrors the outline of its individual dynamic curves. Similarly, the 'Slava', which contains two type (3) curves (bb. 1–86 and 87–228), has its main high region at the end. In contrast, the 'Věruju' h its principal focal point just over half-way through, its central tyn (bb. 120–316) proving to be more powerful than either of truncated ones (bb. 1–119 and 317–99).

Overall organisation

Because of the motivic bias in the literature published previously about the Mass, several of its large-scale organisational elements have so far been overlooked. The most significant of these is the piece's tonal scheme. Surprisingly, most commentators have assumed that the tonal plans of Janáček's works are at best unsophisticated, sometimes even haphazard. This widely held view is summarised in the *New Grove* article: 'Janáček's treatment of tonality was generally instinctive; the tonal plan of a piece is often more the result of his gravitating towards his favourite keys (Db/C♯, Ab) than of large-scale planning. In the mature works a piece seldom ends in the key it began.' (Tyrrell 1985, 26). Of course, the fact that a work changes key does not preclude logical organisation; nobody would argue that the move from G to E in Mahler's Fourth Symphony is not prepared and consolidated. And, in fact, the frequently 'progressive' tonal plans of Janáček's works are invariably lucid. For example, the First String Quartet proceeds from E minor to Ab minor, a succession that is both anticipated by an Ab minor passage in bb. 38–45 of movement I and resolved by a varied repetition of the very same passage in bb. 121–6 of the finale, as well as by a move from E through B and Eb to Ab in the bass line between b. 127 and the end of the finale (Wingfield 1987a, 253–5).

The key scheme of the *Glagolitic Mass* is particularly carefully organised. The tonal centre of the nine-movement structure is Ab minor-major. The whole work begins and ends in Ab major, the Mass proper (excluding the intradas) progressing from a minor seventh on Eb in b. 1 of the 'Úvod' to the tonic triad of Ab minor at the end of the Organ Solo. There are also two principal subsidiary key areas: Fb/E and C. The three main tonal regions, which together make up an augmented triad on Ab, are all a major third apart.

In the first two movements a move from Ab to E is effected. The Intrada consolidates Ab major firmly enough (bb. 36ff.), but the 'Úvod' leads from a minor seventh on Eb (the dominant of Ab) via a dominant seventh on Gb to an emphatic V^{13}–I cadence in E (bb. 70–5). The C region is used to highlight the conflict between Ab and E: when the Intrada begins in C major this key area proves to be a tonicisation of the third degree of the scale of Ab major, whereas when chord I of C makes a prominent reappearance in the 'Úvod' it is swiftly interpreted as the Neapolitan of the dominant of E major (bb. 31–40). Nevertheless, even at this early stage the ultimate triumph of Ab is suggested. The closing bars (48–9) of the Intrada contain a substitute plagal cadence in Ab major (bVI^6-I), in which an enharmonic first-inversion triad of E major moves directly to the tonic triad in root position. Moreover, in the 'Úvod', the three cadential patterns in E major are all preceded by the dominant of Ab minor (bb. 39–40, 70–1 and 72–5), and in bb. 55–61 the enharmonic dominant of E major is actually surrounded by chords V and i of Ab.

From the first chord of the 'Gospodi' to the closing bar of the Organ Solo Ab minor steadily asserts control over E major. The latter's hold on the tonal scheme is loosened slightly in the 'Gospodi'. For, while this third movement ends in E major, it begins by tonicising Ab minor, and it does not initiate a I_4^6-V-I cadence in E until a late stage (b. 56). E major is further weakened by the omission of its leading-note from chord V of the closing cadential pattern (bb. 83–4). But E major does for the moment survive the attempts to dethrone it, partly by enlisting the help of the third principal tonal region, C, whose appearances in bb. 68–70 and 79–82 exploit its Neapolitan relationship with V of E.

E major only just survives Ab minor's determined onslaught in the 'Slava'. Ostensibly, this movement, like the 'Gospodi', outlines two large-scale harmonic motions to E/Fb, one from a second inversion of an Eb major chord, and the other from a first-inversion triad of Ab minor via I of Eb major (bb. 1–86 and 87–228). However, the initial progression appears firmly rooted in Ab minor. The opening I_4^6 of Eb resolves on to chord i of Ab (bb. 57ff.) through an appoggiatura chord on Ab in bb. 28–33 (Ab–Db–F–Bb). After that, I of E/Fb is approached twice, first via II of Ab and later through V of V of i of that key. Hence the Fb major chord in b. 86 can be viewed as VI of Ab minor, the tonic triad of which returns in first inversion in bb. 87–90. The second large-scale harmonic process of the 'Slava' begins by threatening to destabilise E altogether: it actually moves from i^6 of Ab to a tonicising progression (V–I) in Eb major (bb. 180–1). The situation is rescued belatedly by the saturation of bb. 190–6 with V of E and a subsequent thirty-two-bar Coda in which E is embellished, but never threatened. Notwithstanding these valiant efforts, it is possible to interpret the Eb–E progression in bb. 181ff. as a deceptive cadence in Ab minor requiring resolution in a subsequent movement of the Mass.

In the 'Věruju' the tonal scheme of the Mass reaches its crisis point. The first part of the movement is rounded off by a threefold acclamation of the Ab minor triad (bb. 117–19), although this chord is approached via $iv(ii)_5^6$, rather than through its dominant. Next there is a tortuous move to C major, which, for the first time since the Intrada, shows no sign of ceding to V of E; instead, it becomes a modally inflected dominant of F (bb. 162–209). It is just after this point – during the structural peak of the entire Mass – that the tonal balance is tipped irrevocably back in favour of the Ab region (bb. 210–48 in the published score). Because, after a deceptive move to I of Db, a brief reference to chord i of E is eclipsed by a vehement, sustained outburst of Ab minor (bb. 231–48). Having been prolonged for seventeen more bars at a lower degree of intensity, this chord is now consolidated by triads on its dominant and mediant (bb. 269–81).

The next important tonal event in the 'Věruju' appears rather perverse initially: there is a powerful affirmation of V^7 of E major (bb. 309–16). But the strategy behind this apparent reversal soon becomes obvious. In b. 342, I of C returns, after which the move from C through E to Ab at the main focal point of the movement is retraced with an important modification: E leads to the dominant of Ab as opposed to Ab itself. Thus the usual order of Eb and E in the work so far is reversed and a VI–V–i progression in Ab minor is implied. Both the E and C tonal regions are now reinforcing rather than disrupting the tonic–dominant axis. However, in spite of the overwhelming expectation that has been created of a resolution on to i of Ab minor, this chord does not appear. Instead, VI and V of Ab minor are twice reiterated in bb. 381–99 and the movement is left hanging on the dominant of Ab. As a result, the 'Věruju' is the most unstable movement in the Mass in tonal terms; the completion of its closing cadential formula is left for the final four movements of the work, which delineate a stepwise resolution from Eb through E, F and G on to Ab.

The 'Svet' outlines the first two stages of the upward resolution: Eb–E–F. To begin with, second inversion triads of E and Eb are brought into opposition (bb. 1–36). This oscillation develops into a protracted trilateral conflict in bb. 37–136 between E (bb. 37–47 etc.), Eb (e.g. bb. 55–7) and Db/C♯ (bb. 58–63, 82–7 etc.). By b. 137 Eb has temporarily gained the upper hand and an Eb pedal is held throughout bb. 137–78. But in bb. 179–82 V^7 of C suddenly bursts forth (an event highlighted by the timpani), C major ensuing in bb. i–x (see Example 8). The closing stages of the 'Svet' reconcile the three previously conflicting key areas by interpreting Db as the flattened supertonic of C (bb. 179–82 and i–x), and by treating Eb and E as the flat seventh and leading-note of F (bb. xi–xiv and 186–90), all within the framework of an authentic cadence (V^7 of V–V–I) in F major (bb. 179–98). Significantly, this move to F also resolves the massive prolongation of the dominant of F in bb. 162–209 of the 'Věruju'.

Bb. 1–10 of the 'Agneče' swiftly provide the final two steps of the
Eb–E–F–G–Ab resolution by employing G and Ab as the roots of major-
minor-seventh chords. But throughout this movement the hold of Ab is
somewhat precarious: the unadorned root-position triads of Ab minor and
Ab major respectively in bb. 44–6 and 52–3 are approached not via the
dominant, but through chord iv. Thus the ensuing furious Organ Solo –
the end of the Mass proper – is allotted the task of consolidating Ab once
and for all. This movement cancels the tentative Picardy third of bb. 52–3
of the 'Agneče' and affirms Ab minor, principally through a large-scale
authentic cadence in bb. 111–26. It also puts the primacy of Ab over E and
C beyond any doubt by allotting a subordinate role to the E and C regions.
Several times in the Organ Solo a passage begins on I of E but is deflected
towards I of Ab minor; V_2^4 and I of E major even decorate the V–i cadence
in Ab in bb. 111–26. Equally importantly, the concluding cadence
(bb. 146–54) incorporates a final-inversion dominant seventh on C.
Janáček's late decision to add the Organ Solo to the Mass certainly
removed any possible ambiguity from his tonal plan. The function of the
closing Intrada is to re-establish the tonic major, heard at the beginning of
the work and suggested thereafter by several C–Bb–Ab melodic motions
occurring in conjunction with the tonic minor triad – for example, in
bb. 39–46 of the 'Agneče' – and also by the frequent tonicisation of its
mediant (C). In conclusion, it should be noted that the tonal plan of the
published eight-movement version of the Mass is no less logical than that
of the nine-movement arrangement. The initial affirmation of Ab major is
simply omitted, the piece delineating an elaborated version (v–VI–V–i/I) of
the nineteenth-century truncated tonal model (V–I) described on p. 100
above.

Key structure is not the sole dimension in which large-scale organisation
can be discovered in the *Glagolitic Mass*. As with Janáček's other major
1926 work, the Sinfonietta, the movements of the Mass are arranged in an
arch pattern. Five choral movements are framed either side by two instrumental ones, the most substantial and complex movement occupying the
centre of the arch. The first four movements gradually increase in length,
culminating in the massive 'Věruju'; the remaining four movements dim-
inish towards the abrupt final Intrada.[3] The disposition of the dynamic
curves in the Mass is similarly symmetrical. First, the equivalent movements in the ascending and descending parts of the arch have similar
climactic arrangements: the two intradas are identical; the 'Úvod' and
Organ Solo both incorporate a single type (1) curve; the 'Gospodi' and

'Agneče' (both *ABA'*) each contain a type (2) curve; and the 'Slava' and 'Svet' both include two curves, the second of which is more powerful than first. Furthermore, the 'Věruju' – the only movement with three curves – accords precedence to the middle one of the three, the most powerful focal point of the entire Mass (in the equivalent of bb. 210–48 of the published score) thus occurring at the centre of the work.

If we examine another aspect of the Mass's structural peaks – their relative prominence – a powerful, asymmetrical undercurrent to their external arrangement in an arch pattern emerges. There are thirteen highpoints and high regions altogether. The first six increase in impact, a process which culminates in the second high region of the 'Věruju'. Then through curves 8–11 there is an overall (if not absolutely regular) decrease in tension. However, the implied gradual descent from the Mass's principal focal point is interrupted by the twelfth structural peak: the violent culmination of the Organ Solo, whose power vastly surpasses that of any other focal point apart from the second high region of the 'Věruju'. The Organ Solo's dynamic disruption of an initially regular process is one of the most arresting events in the entire Mass.

Word-setting

Janáček set his text for the Mass basically as though it were modern Czech. Thus before an examination of word-setting in the work is undertaken, the principal features of Czech accentuation should be explained. Unlike Church Slavonic, which has movable stress, Czech mainly accentuates the first syllable of a word. Consequently, Czech prose largely comprises a mixture of trochees ($-\ \cup$) and dactyls ($-\ \cup\ \cup$). However, not all trochees and dactyls are equal rhythmically, because of another distinctive feature of Czech: the independence of stress and vowel quantity. Vowels can be long or short, but long ones are not necessarily stressed. For example, in the word 'Sláva', the first 'a' is long and stressed, the second one short and unstressed; whereas in 'Dvořák', the first vowel is short and stressed, the second one long and unstressed. Hence, though these words both have trochaic first-syllable stresses, they have a trochaic ($-\ \cup$) and an iambic ($\cup\ -$) durational pattern respectively. Example 14 shows possible musical representations of both words. An additional complication is that in Czech the stress of non-prepositional monosyllables is flexible, depending on context and emphasis. A phrase beginning with two unstressed monosyllables, for instance, has an initial anapaestic rhythmic pattern ($\cup\ \cup\ -$).

Ex. 14

Thus, in a musical setting of Czech prose iambs and anapaests occur sometimes in the dimension of stress (even if trochees and dactyls predominate), and frequently in the dimension of duration.[4]

By 1926 Janáček had written eight operas and had developed a mainly naturalistic mode of setting Czech prose for solo voices. In *Kát'a*, *Vixen* and *Makropulos*, the motivic structure is controlled by the orchestra, allowing the vocal parts 'to roam freely above it in a more or less realistic stylisation of spoken Czech' (Tyrrell 1988, 297). In the *Glagolitic Mass* too the motivic montage is dominated by the orchestra. The solo voice parts largely either double or embellish instrumental motives, more independent vocal writing being reserved for major textural highpoints (e.g. bb. 54–75 of the 'Gospodi'). Indeed, of the fifty-one principal musical ideas in the work, none remains the exclusive property of the solo voices. Nevertheless, despite the textural similarities between the Mass and the later operas, there are some major differences concerning the style of their solo parts, as can now be demonstrated.

Example 15 shows the solo tenor part from bb. 46–58 of the 'Věruju'. This displays some features of naturalistic Czech (but not Church Slavonic) word-setting: first-syllable stresses are observed on the whole; and triplets are used for words (or groups of words) that would have dactylic patterns in Czech – 'roždena' in b. 57, for example. But this tenor line also has many unrealistic characteristics, even if it is treated as a setting of Czech as opposed to Church Slavonic. Its note values are relatively slow, it incorporates several melismas, and it contains some unnaturalistic stresses – e.g. the placing of the final syllable of 'i-sti-na' on the first beat of a bar (b. 51). Furthermore, its durational patterns essentially do not reflect differences in vowel quantity and there are few repeated notes per melodic unit. In contrast, the solo vocal parts in the later operas have much faster note values on average, they use melismas more sparingly, their stress and durational patterns are proportionally more realistic, and they frequently

113

Ex. 15

depict the rather flat intonation of Czech by employing a substantial number of repeated notes in the setting of each phrase of text.

A yet more significant difference between Example 15 and Janáček's basic late operatic style concerns the relationship between voices and orchestra. In the full score, each of the tenor's utterances shown in Example 15 begin and end simultaneously with instrumental motivic units. Most of the solo vocal interjections in the Mass behave in a similar manner. On the other hand, the more naturalistic solo vocal units in the operas normally start after, and end before, the orchestral ones, their emphasis tending 'to be at the middle of the phrase' (Tyrrell 1988, 296).

The chorus parts in the Mass are even less naturalistic than the solo vocal lines. Although the melodic lines of most of the choral units observe the Czech first-syllable stress rule, virtually all of them simply double or slightly embellish orchestral motives and few have any other realistic features. The accompanying voices of these mainly homophonic units also mostly double instrumental lines; in fact, the word-setting in some of the subsidiary chorus parts is almost completely unnaturalistic (e.g. in bb. 18–25 of the 'Gospodi').

These are two main reasons why the word-setting in the Mass is so different from that in the operas. First, despite the substantial roles for the soprano and tenor soloists (the bass has less to do and the alto barely features), most of the Mass's text is allotted to the chorus, who are largely limited to a few wordless offstage contributions in the later operas; and while fast-moving realistic patter may be idiomatic for solo voices, it is scarcely suitable for 150 or more vocalists singing simultaneously. Second, the text of the Mass does not represent everyday speech, but ritual declamation, which is more stylised. As a result, it was both prudent and appropriate for Janáček to return when writing the Mass to the restrained, predominantly homophonic and minimally naturalistic choral idiom of his two previous works for chorus and orchestra: *Čarták on the Soláň* (1911) and *The Eternal Gospel* (1914).

6

Literature 1927–30

Leoš Janáček in *Lidové noviny* (27 November 1927)

Why did I compose it?

It pours, the Luhačovice rain pours down. From the window I look up to the glowering Komoň mountain.

Clouds roll past; the gale-force wind tears them apart, scatters them far and wide.

Exactly like a month ago: there in front of the Hukvaldy school we stood in the rain.

And next to me the high-ranking ecclesiastical dignitary [Archbishop Prečan].

It grows darker and darker. Already I am looking into the black night; flashes of lightning cut through it.

I switch on the flickering electric light on the high ceiling.

I sketch nothing more than the quiet motive of a desperate frame of mind to the words 'Gospodi pomiluj' [Lord have mercy].

Nothing more than the joyous shout 'Slava, Slava!' [Glory].[1]

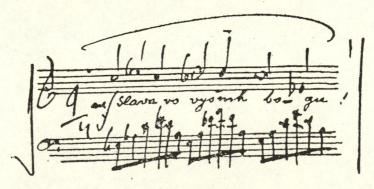

Nothing more than the heart-rending anguish in the motive 'Rozpet že za ny, mŭcen i pogreben jest!' [and was crucified also for us, he suffered and was buried].

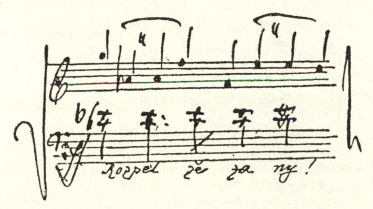

Nothing more than the steadfastness of faith and the swearing of allegiance in the motive 'Věruju!' [I believe].

And all the fervour and excitement of the expressive ending 'Amen, amen!'.

The holy reverence in the motives 'Svät, svät!' [Holy], 'Blagoslovljen' [Blessed] and 'Agneče Božij!' [O Lamb of God].

Without the gloom of mediaeval monastery cells in its motives,
without the sound of the usual imitative procedures,
without the sound of Bachian fugal tangles,
without the sound of Beethovenian pathos,
without Haydn's playfulness;
against the paper barriers of Witt's reforms – which have estranged us from Křížkovský.[2]

Tonight the moon in the lofty canopy lights up my small pieces of paper, full of notes –
tomorrow the sun will steal in inquisitively.

At length the warm air streamed in through the open window into my frozen fingers.

Always the scent of the moist Luhačovice woods – that was the incense.

A cathedral grew before me in the colossal expanse of the hills and the vault of the sky, covered in mist into the distance; its little bells were rung by a flock of sheep.

I hear in the tenor solo some sort of a high priest,
in the soprano solo a maiden-angel,
in the chorus our people.

The candles are high fir trees in the wood, lit up by stars; and in the ritual somewhere out there I see a vision of the princely St Wenceslas.

And the language is that of the missionaries Cyril and Methodius.

And before the evenings of three Luhačovice weeks had flown past, the work was finished; so that Dr Nejedlý was at least partly correct in claiming that I compose like Vymazal: easily and quickly.[3] The 'Glagolskaja missa' will be performed on 5 December at the Stadium in Brno. I praise in advance the singing of Mr Tauber and Mrs Čvanová. Also the few notes – but healthy ones – of Miss Hloušková and Mr Němeček. I praise the fresh voices and secure intonation of the chorus.

Mascagni has already been satisfied with the orchestra and surely the Brno Philharmonic Society will be satisfied with the conductor, Jaroslav Kvapil.

Leoš Janáček to Kamila Stösslová (25 November 1927)

In this work, which will be performed on 5 December, I am representing a bit of the legend about the heavens being torn open when Christ was crucified on the cross. Well then, I depict thunder and flashes of lightning, but if Kamila were to appear in this gateway in the sky – that would be yet more pleasant to portray!

Today I wrote some lines, about how I myself imagine a cathedral. I located it in Luhačovice. That's good, isn't it? Where else could it stand, other than the place where we were so happy! And this cathedral is lofty; it reaches up to the canopy of heaven. And candles burn there; these are tall fir trees, and they are lit up at the top by little stars. And the little bells in the cathedral, those are provided by a flock of sheep. Such is the cathedral depicted in my work for 5. XII.

But as for now. Two people enter this cathedral, marching ceremonially along a fully carpeted path of green grass. And these two wish to be married. Oddly, the two are still alone. O priest, do please arrive! Nightingales, thrushes, ducks and geese make the music! Indeed, the chief among them wants to take for himself the gentle little black-haired one – dear Kamila.

End of dream. You are already sleeping and I am in ecstasy about you.

Václav Kaprál in *Hudební rozhledy* (15 February 1928)

The Old Church Slavonic mass text is evidently only the superficial framework for Janáček's distinctive mode of utterance. In this work Janáček expresses a relationship to God that I would describe as pantheistic. He avoids all things ecclesiastical; instead, a vivified nature-god sings his paean of praise to the Most High. Directness, terseness and expressiveness, those typical Janáčekian characteristics, form the fundamental basis of Janáček's compositional method, even for such an unusual subject as this. The opening and concluding intradas of the Mass, sparklingly orchestrated and strongly tinged with folk colour, are traditional insertions. Of the individual movements, which are all original in conception, the Credo is especially outstanding. The organ solo's novel mode of utterance is also arresting. Here we see best of all how Janáček exploits to the full the colour and expressional capabilities of every instrument. The originality of this Mass will surely create a great sensation abroad. The performance by the Brno Philharmonic Society under Kvapil's guidance was executed quite brilliantly as far as the chorus was concerned. Only the orchestra of the National Theatre still needed to have had at least one more rehearsal.

Ludvík Kundera in the Prague periodical *Tempo* (February 1928)

The *Glagolitic Mass* has the following philosophical basis. Janáček, an old man, now a firm believer, feels with increasing urgency that his life's work should not lack an element expressing his relationship to God . . . To this end the Mass text serves him best, as with so many composers before him. Also, this text is quite heterogeneous and gives the composer the opportunity to unfold the most diverse of moods: in the humble and despairing Kyrie, the joyous Gloria, the dramatically animated and emotionally varied Credo, and then in the lyrical parts of the Mass – the Sanctus, Benedictus and Agnus.

Of course, Janáček does not see his God in terms of the mystical twilight of the altar, as the glow of a monstrance, enveloped by the scent of incense, but – and this is characteristic of the composer – imagines him outside in the open air . . .

Leoš Janáček in *Literární svět* (8 March 1928)

The Old Church Slavonic Mass? You know what they [Kundera] wrote about me: 'an old man, now a believer'. But this only annoyed me and I said: 'You youngster, for one thing I am no old man, and I am not at all a believer; no, not at all. Until I see for myself.' It has occurred to me that the year 1928 is lacking something: what is missing is a Cyrillo-Methodian atmosphere, which is why I want to associate my work with this year [the tenth anniversary of Czechoslovak independence]. In fact, I have had the piece ready since 1926. I wrote it in Luhačovice; it was dreadful there.

Rain poured down day after day, and each evening I sat down and adhered to a strict routine; in three weeks the work was finished.[4] In it I wanted to portray faith in the certainty of the nation, not on a religious basis, but on a strong moral foundation which calls God as a witness.

William Ritter in the *Gazette de Lausanne* (18 March 1928)

The premiere in Brno (Brunn) of this impassioned and unexpected work, truly created from lava and fire, caused the greatest artistic stir of our last [Czecho]slovak tour. And this was as much a surprise for the Czech musical world as for us . . .

It is a bellicose and militant Mass, in which we sometimes have the impression of the mounting of an assault on the celestial redoubts, sometimes of naive prayers, of popular supplications tinged with a frenetic tenderness, and above all of a secular tone as yet never heard in church. Ah, it is not humble this Mass . . . It attacks the Thrones and the Dominations,[5] and occasionally the convulsive energy that animates it makes one think rather of Dantesque Gemoniae.[6]

With all this there is a Kyrie (a figure of speech, since 'Gospodine pomiluje' is sung)[7] in which we believe that we hear the real and eternal distress of the Russian people; a Gloria which is the most beautiful of Slav pastorales, with the flutes of shepherds each robed in a 'halena' (smock) and the rippling of [Czecho]slovak streams beneath the stormy skies of Valhalla, all in the style of a popular crib; a furibund Sanctus, a seismological Credo.[8] As for the Agnus Dei – I continue to employ traditional terminology – it is one of those effusions that could only be produced by those who have sinned greatly, but of whom much will be forgiven for the familiar reason. Finally, there is an organ Intrada – to accompany the exit; the faithful pour out of the church as if through a monumental rustic triumphal arch.[9]

Erich Steinhard in *Der Auftakt* (1929, 114)

Of the large-scale vocal works [performed at the 1929 ISCM Festival in Geneva], L. Janáček's 'Missa Glagolskaja' undisputedly made the strongest impact. One heard naive listeners asking: 'Should a Mass be like that?' Of course, it is indeed the Mass of a naive man. It certainly has nothing to do with the church, the clergy or mysticism. Rather it is a rustic Mass of unheard-of power . . . The whole Mass is a hymn of rejoicing, with fanfares at the beginning and the end. A worldly victory celebration in the Old Slavonic vernacular. The music is operatic. The Credo is joyfully passionate [*sic*], the Gloria cheerful, the Sanctus and Benedictus purely dramatic. Several motives sound as though they have been taken from his operas; other features that point to an operatic type of language are the Vivace treatment of the 'Amen', the naturalistic handling of the chorus and the emotionally charged virtuoso piece, the mighty organ movement at the end. Power, force, wildness, shouting up to heaven.

Rosa Newmarch in the programme for the Triennial Norwich Festival (23 October 1930)

The fundamental idea of his Mass, which dates from 1926–7, was as much patriotic as pious: something of the impulse which caused Brahms to write his *German Requiem*. The actual title of the work – a *Glagolitic Mass* – supports this view.

Apart from patriotic feeling, the varied emotional content of the Mass, dramatic and lyrical, must have offered a strong attraction to the composer. The element which struck him most forcibly was that of ecstatic joy. Had he attached a motto to his score, it must have been some jubilant quotations from the Psalms of David, such as: 'God is gone up with a shout', or 'Let him praise His Name in the dance'.

Harold Truscott in the *Yorkshire Post* (24 October 1930)

Janáček's Mass is not an absolute novelty, but this was its first performance in England . . . One has to shed all one's prejudices in favour of civilised European music, German or Italian, to appreciate its virtues. It has to be taken as the exuberant joy of a primitive folk on a popular festival, of a people whose simple faith allows them to be on terms of intimacy with Divine things, and to whom the awe and reserve of Northern temperaments are unknown.

The work is perhaps hardly in its right place in a sedate English concert, set to English words which do not fit it, and one feels that 'Lord, have mercy' would sound much better in the original. It is not likely that this extraordinary work will ever be acclimatised here . . .

Ferruccio Bonavia in the *Musical Times* (1 December 1930)

Janáček's 'Slavonic' Mass does purport to be something more than a musical representation of the sacrament known as the Mass. According to a note by Mrs Rosa Newmarch, the composer was drawn to the theme by 'patriotic feeling, emotional content, dramatic and lyrical'; but patriotism predominates and informs the whole. He calls his work a 'Glagolitic' Mass, thus connecting it with the Glagolitic alphabet of St Methodius – a title which the publishers have since altered, since they allege, it conveys nothing to the general public. That might be an excellent reason for retaining it; for, to the average listener, the music conveys no more than the title. Let me say quite frankly that I found the score not only futile as music, but even irreverent, since this attempt to blend the words that form the text of the Mass with music whose best description is contained in the programme – 'God is gone up with a shout' – seems to be completely irresponsible.

What impression this work can make on the followers of St Methodius I cannot imagine, but I noticed that when the chorus emitted a series of hasty 'Amens' closely resembling in speed and accent the perfunctory 'All right' of a creditor to a pleading debtor, every face in the Norwich audience was wreathed in smiles. If there were weak moments in performance, the performers nevertheless had all my sympathy.

It is fully probable that Janáček speaks a language that his countrymen alone understand. If this is indeed the case it seems a pity to export an article clearly intended for home consumption.

Olin Downes in the *New York Times* (27 October 1930)

This Mass . . . is great and partly incoherent music. It is so different from a Roman mass that its crude, primitive, Hussite conception of the ritual will shock the esthetic sensibilities of many people wholly unprepared for it, as it will merely puzzle or bore others. It is very stark, barbaric stuff. Steel rings in the music, and ancient racial voices . . .

Meanwhile, although there are suggestions of Moussorgsky and perhaps of other composers that Janáček knew and subconsciously sympathized with, the music is fantastically, impractically, and inarticulately original. Sometimes one thinks a little of Bruckner, Janáček's master [?], in the reiteration of certain musical figures. But this is a parallel rather than a tendency held by the two in common. Janáček's thinking is wholly different

from Bruckner's in this work, which is certainly the truest and most original expression of his genius that is known to us. (The opera *Jenůfa*, performed in a recent season by the Metropolitan Opera Company, is much less creative.)

Janáček writes almost entirely in a harmonic style, dispensing with the old contrapuntal forms and nearly all of their devices. He writes harmonic combinations which are not suggested or endorsed by anybody. Solo and choral passages are harmonically so bold and uncompromising that, lacking the printed music, the listener might well wonder if the musicians were not wholly mistaken or miraculously off pitch and key with each other. Yet the logic of this procedure is clear, even if it is not practical in sonorous effect or organic in the accepted harmonic sense . . . Similar unpredictable originalities are found in the instrumentation, which has sometimes a wonderful brilliancy and glow – veritable bursts of color – of its own. In other passages, it is wholly ineffective, almost ridiculous, for thinness and poor spacing.

The same thing in invention. Sometimes, in a magnificent burst, the composer takes an amazing flight. Then he suddenly seems to halt, perplexed, entirely at sea. Then he fumbles about, manipulates some formula or other, dwells upon an idea which leads nowhere, till light breaks again and once more, heroically, prophetically, he soars to the sun.

The form of the mass is wholly unconventional. The conclusion no more follows tradition, with its organ and orchestra postludia, than anything else in the piece. This is a huge, tremendous work, a conception only half expressed; one which only partly realizes a vision that must have dazzled the composer. This composition can hardly hope for success with the public or a permanent place in the repertory, which, concretely speaking, it does not seem to deserve. But it is an inspiring composition.

Notes

1 Genesis and reception

1 See Wingfield 1987a for details of Janáček's reuse of material from his earlier Piano Trio (1908–9) in the initial draft of the First String Quartet (1923–4).
2 Further information about the 1907–8 Mass is supplied in Petrželka 1946, Firkušný 1946 (120–1), Gardavský 1955 and Vogel 1963 (146–8). Petrželka's completion of the Credo is considered briefly in Wingfield 1988.
3 The four letters concerning the Mass of 2, 3, 4 and 14 September are housed in the Janáček Archive, which forms part of the Music History Division of the Moravian Museum in Brno. They have the following class marks: A 3582, A 4698, B 904 and A 801.
4 Janáček Archive A 5665.
5 The full Czech text of the article is in Firkušný and Racek 1958, 57–61; other English translations can be found in V. and M. Tausky 1982, 52–5, and Zemanová 1989, 111–14.
6 The dates of these rehearsals can be calculated from three unpublished letters written by Janáček to Kamila (Janáček Archive E 515, E 6 and E 516) – see Wingfield 1987b, 187–8.
7 William Ritter (1867–1955) wrote extensively about Czechoslovak music and corresponded with Janáček in the period 1924–8. His 17 December 1926 letter is printed in Racek and Rektorys 1953, 261–2; an English translation is in Susskind 1985, 116–17.
8 Janáček Archive E 516.
9 This letter is held by the Schweizerische Landesbibliothek in Berne.
10 An English translation of the whole of this interview can be found in Zemanová 1989, 120–4.
11 Also held by the Schweizerische Landesbibliothek.
12 Janáček Archive A 4769.

2 The (Old?) Church Slavonic text

1 It should be noted that 'i' after another vowel ('post-vocalic i') is always written as a 'j' according to probable OCS pronunciation: hence 'uj' in 'pomiluj'. Dvorník 1956 and 1970 are the most accessible accounts of early Slavic history and of the Moravian mission. Nandriş 1959, Lunt 1974 and Gardiner 1984 are indispensable OCS grammars; Kurz and others 1966– and Lysaght 1978 are the main dictionaries of OCS. Auty 1960 contains a wide selection of Glagolitic and Cyrillic OCS texts in the original scripts.
2 Vajs 1948, 56–158, describes Illirico 4 fully; Plates i–vi of Vajs's book reproduce fols. 166–8 of the manuscript.

3 The authentic score

1 For further details of unauthorised recomposition in Janáček's music see, for example, Wingfield 1987b, 169–213.

2 Janáček Archive E 518.
3 To avoid ambiguity, the terms 'climax', 'climactic' etc. are employed exclusively to denote the arrangement of important structural events in ascending order of intensity; the apex of such a process is labelled 'highpoint' or, if more protracted in length, 'high region'. This terminology is derived from Agawu 1984.
4 Fol. 118v of Janáček Archive A 7447.
5 In his unfinished orchestral work *The Danube* (1923–8), Janáček also places important motivic and harmonic material in up to four sets of pedal timpani at some points. He quotes two of the motives involving several sets of timpani in his autobiography (Veselý 1924, 98).

4 Synopsis

1 This chapter and the next observe the 1927–8 nine-movement arrangement of the work described on p. 53.
2 For the sake of conciseness, this chapter uses the label 'motive' to indicate both a short melodic unit on its own and a short melodic unit plus its accompanying lines. It is always clear from the context which definition of the term is being employed. Chapter 5 uses only the first definition.
3 Half-diminished seventh – a seventh chord comprising the following intervals in relation to the bass: minor third, diminished fifth, minor seventh.
4 Interestingly, this organ motive is almost identical with that employed in the piano cadenza (bb. 168–93) of the final movement of the Capriccio, which Janáček completed around the time that he wrote the Organ Solo – see p. 11.
5 Major-minor seventh – a seventh chord comprising the following intervals in relation to the bass: minor third, perfect fifth, major seventh.

5 Introduction to the musical organisation

1 A unit is deemed to consist of two identical or similar parts only if internal repetition occurs in the vast majority of its subsequent statements.
2 V^0_8: a dominant minor ninth with its root omitted.
3 A cursory glance at the score might suggest that the Organ Solo lasts longer than the 'Agneče', because it has more bars. However, the slower tempo marking of the 'Agneče' means that it is in fact about twice as long as the Organ Solo.
4 See Tyrrell 1988, 254–8, for a fuller discussion of Czech stress patterns.

6 Literature 1927–30

1 Surprisingly, none of the musical examples in this article is an exact quotation from the Mass. For instance, the first one sets the opening line of the text of the 'Slava' to a flute and oboe variant of the main motive from b. 9 of that movement, employing an accompanimental figure from b. 10 and transposing all the notes up a tone. The fifth example even combines variants of motives from the 'Věruju' and 'Svet'. Similarly, the Church Slavonic text here is inaccurate: 'rozpet' derives from Janáček's autograph, but 'jest' is simply wrong. Presumably, the composer quoted both the text and the music from memory when writing this article and neglected to check either.
2 Pavel Křížkovský (1820–85), a leading Moravian composer of choral music, was Janáček's teacher and choirmaster at the Augustinian 'Queen's' monastery in Brno in 1865–9.
3 Zdeněk Nejedlý (1878–1962) was one of the principal founders of Czech musicology; František Vymazal (1841–1917), a Brno polyglot, published grammars of most foreign languages with the motto 'easily and quickly'.

4 Only the first draft was completed in Luhačovice – see p. 10.
5 The 'Thrones' and 'Dominations' are the third and fourth of the nine orders of angels enumerated in the fifth-century Pseudo-Dionysian *Areopagita*.
6 The 'Gemoniae' were the steps on the Aventine Hill in Rome leading to the Tiber to which the bodies of executed criminals were dragged to be thrown into the river. The word is misapplied figuratively here in the sense of 'tortures'.
7 'Gospodine pomiluje' is not sung in any source or edition of the Mass.
8 Ritter's ethnographic terminology is confused: apart from insisting on calling the whole of Czechoslovakia 'Slovakia', he uses 'Slav' and 'Russian' interchangeably.
9 Ritter conflates the final two movements into one.

Principal sources of the *Glagolitic Mass*

Manuscripts

Date	Location	Signature	Contents
1926	Janáček Archive	A 7447	Janáček's two incomplete early drafts and full autograph
1926	Österreichische Nationalbibliothek	L1UE 223	Sedláček's authorised copy containing a copy of the printed 1920 *Cyril* text
1927	Janáček Archive	A 49.308	Kulhánek's authorised copy
1927	Brno State Philharmonic Archive	Not catalogued	Incomplete set of manuscript string and chorus parts

Printed editions

Date	Type	UE No.	Remarks
1928	Vocal score	9544	Piano arrangement by Ludvík Kundera; underlaid Church Slavonic and German texts
1929	Full score	9541	Underlaid Church Slavonic and German texts
1930	Vocal score	9544	Revised with a new introduction by Miloš Weingart and English and Latin texts (not underlaid)
1956	Pocket full score	13 366	
1969	Vocal score	9544a	Underlaid English and Latin texts

Bibliography

Agawu, Kofi. 1984. 'Structural "Highpoints" in Schumann's *Dichterliebe*', *Music Analysis*, 3, 156–80

Auty, Robert. 1960. *Handbook of Old Church Slavonic Grammar, Part II: Texts and Glossary*. London

Bent, Ian and William Drabkin. 1987. *The New Grove Handbooks in Music: Analysis*. London

Birnbaum, Henrik. 1981. 'Eastern and Western Components in the Earliest Slavic Liturgy', in *Essays in Early Slavic Civilisation*, 36–51. Munich

Blážek, Vilém. 1969. 'K premiéře Janáčkovy Glagolské mše' [On the Premiere of Janáček's *Glagolitic Mass*], *Hudební rozhledy*, 22, 684–5

1971. 'Neznámé marginálie Leoše Janáčka' [Leoš Janáček's unknown marginalia], *Opus musicum*, 3, 112–13

Černušák, Gracián and others. 1960. *Sto let Filharmonického sboru besedy brněnské* [One Hundred Years of the Philharmonic Chorus of the Brno Friendly Society]. Brno

Dahlhaus, Carl. 1985. *Realism in Nineteenth-century Music*, trans. Mary Whittall. Cambridge

Dvorník, Francis. 1956. *The Slavs: Their Early History and Civilisation*. Boston

1970. *Byzantine Missions Among the Slavs: SS. Constantine-Cyril and Methodius*. New Brunswick, New Jersey

Firkušný, Leoš. 1946. *Vilém Petrželka*. Prague

Firkušný, Leoš and Jan Racek, eds. 1958. *Leoš Janáček: fejetony z Lidových novin*, rev. 2nd edn. Brno

Gardavský, Čeněk. 1955. 'Chrámové a varhanní skladby Leoše Janáčka' [Leoš Janáček's Church and Organ Compositions], *Musikologie*, 3, 330–42

Gardiner, Sunray. 1984. *Old Church Slavonic: an Elementary Grammar*. Cambridge

Haefeli, Anton. 1982. *Die Internationale Gesellschaft für Neue Musik (IGNM): Ihre Geschichte von 1922 bis zur Gegenwart*. Zurich

Hollander, Hans. 1963. 'Das monothematische Prinzip der Glagolitischen Messe', in *Leoš Janáček a soudobá hudba: mezinárodní hudebně vědecký kongres, Brno 1958* [Janáček and Contemporary Music: International Musicological Conference, Brno 1958], 129–31. Prague

Kurz, Josef and others, eds. 1966–. *Slovník Jazyka Staroslověnského* [Dictionary of the Old Church Slavonic Language]. Prague

Lunt, Horace. 1974. *Old Church Slavonic Grammar*, rev. 6th edn. The Hague

Lysaght, Thomas. 1978. *Material Towards the Compilation of a Concise Old Church Slavonic–English Dictionary*. Wellington

Mareš, Francis. 1985. 'A Basic Reform of the Orthography at the Early Period of Croatian–Glagolitic Church Slavonic', in *The Formation of the Slavonic Literary Languages*, ed. Gerald Stone and Dean Worth, 177–81. Columbus, Ohio

Nandriş, Grigore. 1959. *Handbook of Old Church Slavonic, Part I: Old Church Slavonic Grammar*. London

Petrželka, Vilém. 1946. Introduction to the Hudební matice edition (no. 1177) of Leoš Janáček's unfinished Mass in Eb

Quioka, Rudolf. 1964. 'Über den Cäcilianismus-Cyrilismus in Böhmen', *Kirchenmusikalisches Jahrbuch*, 48, 143–53

Racek, Jan. 1975. *Leoš Janáček v mých vzpomínkách* [Leoš Janáček as I Remember him]. Prague

Racek, Jan and Artuš Rektorys, eds. 1953. *Korespondence Leoše Janáčka s Maxem Brodem* [Leoš Janáček's Correspondence with Max Brod]. Prague

Ratner, Leonard. 1966. *Music: The Listener's Art*, rev. 2nd edn. New York

Schoenberg, Arnold. 1967. *Fundamentals of Musical Composition*, ed. Gerald Strang and Leonard Stein. London

Simpson, Adrienne. 1982. '"Kát'a Kabanová" in the United Kingdom', in John Tyrrell, *Leoš Janáček: Kát'a Kabanová*, 120–8. Cambridge

Štědroň, Bohumír. 1953. 'Janáčkovy "Listy důvěrné"' [Janáček's 'Intimate Letters'], *Hudební rozhledy*, 6, 608–18

1976. *Leoš Janáček*. Prague

Ströbel, Dietmar. 1975. *Motiv und Figur in den Kompositionen der Jenůfa-Werkgruppe Leoš Janáčeks*. Munich and Salzburg

Susskind, Charles. 1985. *Janáček and Brod*. New Haven

Tausky, Vilem and Margaret, eds. 1982. *Leoš Janáček: Leaves from his Life*. London

Tyrrell, John. 1980. Disc notes to the Decca recording of *From the House of the Dead*, conducted by Charles Mackerras, D224D 2

1982. *Leoš Janáček: Kát'a Kabanová*. Cambridge

1985. 'Leoš Janáček', in *The New Grove: Turn of the Century Masters*, ed. Stanley Sadie, 1–77. London

1988. *Czech Opera*. Cambridge

Vajs, Josef. 1948. *Najstariji Hrvatskoglagoļski misal* [The Oldest Croatian–Glagolitic Missal]. Zagreb

Večerka, Radoslav. 1957. 'K historii textu Janáčkovy Hlaholské mše' [On the History of the Text of Janáček's *Glagolitic Mass*], *Sborník prací filosofické fakulty brněnské university*, F1, 64–76

Veselý, Adolf, ed. 1924. *Leoš Janáček: pohled do života i díla* [Leoš Janáček: A View of the Life and Works]. Prague

Vogel, Jaroslav. 1963. *Leoš Janáček: život a dílo* [Leoš Janáček: Life and Works]. Prague

Bibliography

Weingart, Miloš. 1930. 'Bemerkungen zum Glagolitischen und Lateinischen Text', preface to the Universal Edition revised vocal score of the *Glagolitic Mass* (no. 9544)

Wingfield, Paul. 1987a. 'Janáček's Lost "Kreutzer" Sonata', *Journal of the Royal Musical Association*, 112/2, 229–56

1987b. 'Source Problems in Janáček's Music: Their Significance and Interpretation'. Diss., U. of Cambridge

1988. Disc notes to the EMI recording of Janáček's Unfinished Mass in Eb, conducted by Stephen Cleobury, CDC 749092 2

Wörner, Karl. 1969. 'Leoš Janáček', in *Das Zeitalter der thematischen Prozesse in der Geschichte der Musik*, 146–53. Regensburg

Zemanová, Mirka. 1989. *Janáček's Uncollected Essays on Music*. London

Index